CHRONOLOGY AND DOCUMENTARY HANDBOOK OF THE STATE OF
COLORADO

MARY L. FRECH,

State Editor

WILLIAM F. SWINDLER,

Series Editor

1973 OCEANA PUBLICATIONS, INC./ Dobbs Ferry, New York

This is Volume 6 in the series CHRONOLOGIES AND DOCUMENTARY HANDBOOKS OF THE STATES.

HOUSTON PUBLIC LIBRARY

© Copyright 1973 by Oceana Publications, Inc.

Library of Congress Cataloging in Publication Data
Main entry under title:

Chronology and documentary handbook of the State of
   Colorado.

(Chronologies and documentary handbooks of the
states, v. 6)
   SUMMARY: Includes a chronology of events in
Colorado from 1706 to 1971, a biographical directory,
an outline of the state Constitution, and selected
documents.
   Bibliography: p.
   1. Colorado--History--Chronology. 2. Colorado--
History--Sources. [1. Colorado--History] I. Frech,
Mary L,, ed. II. Series.
F776.C5   978.8   73-532

ISBN 0-379-16131-1

Manufactured in the United States of America

CONTENTS

INTRODUCTION v
CHRONOLOGY (1706-1971) 1
BIOGRAPHICAL DIRECTORY 17
OUTLINE OF CONSTITUTION 25
SELECTED DOCUMENTS 31
    A Lady's Life in the Rocky Mountains 33
    Colorado and Its Capitol 59
    The Juvenile Court 75
SELECTED BIBLIOGRAPHY 103
NAME INDEX 105

INTRODUCTION

This projected series of *Chronologies and Documentary Handbooks of the States* will ultimately comprise fifty separate volumes – one for each of the states of the Union. Each volume is intended to provide a concise ready reference of basic data on the state, and to serve as a starting point for more extended study as the individual user may require. Hopefully, it will be a guidebook for a better informed citizenry – students, civic and service organizations, professional and business personnel, and others.

The editorial plan for the *Handbook* series falls into five divisions: (1) a chronology of selected events in the history of the state; (2) a short biographical directory of the principal public officials, e.g., governors, Senators and Representatives; (3) an analytical outline of the state constitution; (4) the text of some representative documents illustrating main currents in the political, economic, social or cultural history of the state; and (5) a selected bibliography for those seeking further or more detailed information. Most of the data found in the present volume, in fact, have been taken from one or another of these references.

The user of these *Handbooks* may ask why the full text of the state constitution, or the text of constitutional documents which affected the history of the state, have not been included. There are several reasons: In the case of the current constitution, the text in almost all cases is readily available from one or more official agencies within the state. In addition, the current constitutions of all fifty states, as well as the federal Constitution, are regularly kept up to date in the definitive collection maintained by the Legislative Drafting Research Fund of Columbia University and published by the publisher of the present series of *Handbooks*. These texts are available in most major libraries under the title, *Constitutions of the United States: National and State*, in two volumes, with a companion volume, the *Index Digest of State Constitutions*.

Finally, the complete collection of documents illustrative of the constitutional development of each state, from colonial or territorial status up to the current constitution as found in the Columbia University collection, is being prepared for publication in a multi-volume series by the present series editor. Whereas the present series of *Handbooks* is intended for a wide range of interested citizens, the series of annotated constitutional materials in the volumes of *Sources and Documents of U.S. Constitutions* is primarily for the specialist in government, history or law. This is not to suggest that the general citizenry may not profit equally from referring to these materials; rather, it points up the separate purpose of the *Handbooks*, which is to guide the user to these and other sources of authoritative information with which he may systematically enrich his knowledge of this state and its place in the American Union.

William F. Swindler
Series Editor

CHRONOLOGY

1706   The Spanish explorer Ulibarri reached the upper Arkansas River, named the general region Santo Domingo, and claimed it for Spain. Although earlier *conquistadores* may have crossed part of this region, this was the first formal notice of territorial jurisdiction by Spanish authority.

1739   Two French explorers, the Mallet brothers, crossed southeastern part of present Colorado en route from Missouri River to Santa Fe.

1776   *August 5.* Father Francisco Escalante led exploring party through south central and southwestern part of present Colorado.

1803   Louisiana Purchase included northeastern part of Colorado, with Arkansas River later fixed as general dividing line from Spanish territory.

1806   *July 15.* Lt. Zebulon M. Pike left St. Louis with small exploring party which reached site of present Pueblo November 23. Expedition discovered "Grand Peak," later named for Pike, and Royal Gorge before being captured by Spanish forces and escorted to Santa Fe.

1818   Madeiro Gonzales Lupton, Spanish employee of American Fur Company, established one of first trading posts on South Platte River.

1819   *May 30.* Major Stephen H. Long left Pittsburgh with party of naturalists to renew exploration of Colorado area. On June 30, expedition sighted and named Long's Peak. Dr. Edwin James, expedition geologist, later climbed "Grand Peak," which was first named for him; with travelers persisting in calling it Pike's Peak, however, James' name was transferred to another mountain.

1829   Four <u>Bent</u> brothers--<u>Charles</u>, <u>George</u>, <u>Robert</u>, and <u>William</u>--constructed large fort near present city of La Junta. This was one of the most successful of a number of trading posts founded in eastern Colorado and among foothills of Rocky Mountains in this period.

1838   <u>Col. Cerean St. Vrain</u> built trading post on South Platte River; it became an important link in a chain extending from Laramie to Bent's Fort.

1840   Town of Pueblo begun with establishment of "buffalo farm" to supply buffalo to eastern zoos, by well-known local trader, "<u>Uncle Dick</u>" Wooton.

1853   <u>Captain J.W. Gunnison</u> explored central Rockies for possible railroad route, later crossing into Utah where he was killed by Piaute Indians.

1858   First discoveries of gold near Cherry Creek made by group of Georgia prospectors, the W. Green Russell Company. First tent and log cabin communities established in vicinity of Denver, named for Kansas Territorial <u>Governor James W. Denver</u>.

April 11. Confident that increasing number of gold discoveries would bring large population to area, settlers called for convention to establish local government and make preparations to petition for statehood.

November 6. Constitution for a provisional "Territory of Jefferson" having been adopted, delegates were dispatched to Washington and to Kansas legislature to seek separate territorial organization. Distance from Kansas settlements, and need of mining districts for courts able to apply laws based on local practice, were primary considerations. R.W. Steele was elected first governor of "Jefferson Territory" and called first session of a territorial legislature following year.

1859

January 7. George A. Jackson discovered rich gold deposit near Idaho Springs. When first major diggings were made by Jackson's Chicago associates in April, stream where discovery was made was named Chicago Creek.

April 23. First newspaper, *Rocky Mountain News,* begun by William N. Byers.

May 6. John Gregory and companions made second major gold discovery at "Gregory diggings" near present day Golden. By summer thousands of prospectors were moving into Colorado area in "Pike's Peak gold rush." Following example of California gold rush, mining districts set up local courts and drafted their own laws for orderly administration of claims and local needs.

October 3. First school opened in Denver.

1860

Rough census for area fixed population at 34,277. Other estimates, however, reduced this figure by about one-third. Practical difficulties of counting a highly mobile population in inaccessible mountain areas, together with hopeless division of jurisdiction between "Jefferson Territory" and Kansas Territory, made all functions of government subject to controversy.

April 5. Towns of Denver and Auraria formally merged.

April 9. Pony express began service from Missouri to California via Denver.

June. System of irrigated farming in area east of Rockies became general, providing a broadened economic base for the whole region.

1861

February 28. Bill organizing separate Territory of Colorado signed by President James Buchanan. Territory was created out of parts of Utah, New Mexico, Kansas, and Nebraska Territories.

April 24. Question of secession or union discussed at mass meeting in Denver, which overwhelmingly voted to keep new territory in the union.

May 20. William Gilpin of Missouri, a veteran western traveler and writer, was appointed as first governor of Colorado Territory. Governor Steele of "Jefferson Territory" formally turned over records of his administration to the new governor and pronounced the end of the provisional government.

September 9. First legislature met in Denver, created nineteen new counties and designated Colorado City as site of territorial capital. New counties included Arapahoe, part of which had been westernmost county of former Kansas Territory; Boulder; Carbonate; Clear Creek; Costilla (Spanish for "rib); Douglas, named for Stephen A. Douglas; El Paso; Fremont, named for John Charles Fremont; Gilpin, named for the first governor; Guadalupe; Huerfano (Spanish for "orphan," suggested by isolated butte in Huerfano River); Jefferson, named for Thomas Jefferson and in memory of the late "territory"; Lake;

Larimer, named for General William Larimer, pioneer and Indian fighter; Park; Pueblo; San Miguel; Summit; and Weld, named for Lewis L. Weld, first secretary of the territory.

1862 *March 26.* Colorado troops formed part of Union force which engaged Confederates at La Glorieta pass in north New Mexico. Defeat of Confederate attempt to seize western plains and eastern Rockies was only Civil War battle involving new territory.

July 11. Second session of legislature moved capital back to Denver, then selected Golden as new site for capital. John Evans of Illinois succeeded Gilpin as governor.

Congress passed Legal Tender Act, establishing government purchases of gold and silver and thus offering new stable market to aid economy of region.

1864 *March 21.* Congress passed enabling act authorizing territorial convention to draft a preliminary to petition for statehood.

May 20. Cherry Creek flood devastated portions of Denver.

July 4. Constitutional convention opened at Golden. It adjourned week later after drafting constitution and ordinances.

July 26. Band of Texas guerillas raided parts of southern Colorado, in one of last engagements of Civil War.

November 29. Sand Creek massacre of 500 Indians by territorial troops touched off violent uprising of mountain and plains Indians.

1865   *August 12.* The 1864 constitution had been rejected in the popular vote the previous year, and on this date a new convention assembled in Denver to make some minor changes in the document and resubmit it for a new vote. The action was widely criticized as illegal, but a group eager for statehood conducted a vigorous propaganda campaign for an affirmative vote. In September the 1865 draft carried by a margin of 155 affirmative votes.

1866   *February 9.* Territorial legislature created Las Animas county (from Spanish for El Rio de las Animas Perdidas en Purgatorio).

May 3. Congress passed bill proposing to admit Colorado to statehood on basis of 1865 constitution, in face of violent objections that action of second convention had had no legal basis.

May 15. President Andrew Johnson vetoed Colorado statehood bill, basing his decision on the doubtful legality of the constitution, the narrow margin of the affirmative vote, and the evidence that, with the exhaustion of the first gold deposits and the depredations of the Indian wars, the territory was steadily losing population. The veto was sustained.

1867   *January 29.* President Johnson vetoed second act of admission to statehood, for same reasons given in his veto message of the previous year.

Denver finally was designated the permanent territorial capital.

Release of a number of military units from former Confederate areas for duty in the plains wars brought relief to territorial forces engaged in various Indian attacks.

CHRONOLOGY

August 23. First successful attempt to reach summit of Long's Peak

1868   Nathaniel Hill constructed smelter at Blackhawk, making possible development of hard ore mining and opening new era in economic growth of territory.

September 17. Nine-day Battle of Beecher's Island began with siege of fifty scouts by several hundred Indians led by Chief Roman Nose. Federal troops eventually relieved the defenders and defeated Indians.

1869   German Colonization Society organized in Chicago to establish first of series of "colony towns" in Colorado, small cooperative agricultural communities operating joint irrigation projects. Although several such ventures failed, others succeeded in establishing towns of Longmont, Platteville, and Fort Collins.

1870   Census showed territorial population of 39,864. This was little more than 5,000 more than the most optimistic figures of 1860 and corroborated general belief that territory had sustained serious losses in population after first gold rush and crisis of Indian wars.

February 11. Bent county created, named for William Bent, one of brothers who established Bent's Fort.

June 24. First railroads, the Denver Pacific and the Kansas Pacific, reached Denver. With the coming of rail connections, the territory began to grow rapidly, the trains bringing in settlers and carrying out agricultural and mineral products to eastern markets.

1871	Colorado Springs founded by General William J. Palmer and associates.

Railroads began extending south from Denver connecting with Central City and Pueblo by end of following year. |
| 1872 | *January 9.* Colorado Stock Growers Association formed. Cattle and sheep raising, an important new agricultural resource, often conflicted with interests of irrigation farmers but nevertheless added to diversified economy of territory. |
| 1873 | Fresh gold and silver discoveries in San Juan mountains led to new rush of miners to southwestern Colorado and brought pressure on Federal government to extinguish Ute Indian titles to land in that area. |
| 1874 | *February 2.* Elbert and Grand counties established; former named for Samuel H. Elbert, sixth territorial governor and chief justice of territorial supreme court.

February 10. Three more counties established: Hinsdale (for Lt. Gov. George A. Hinsdale), La Plata (Spanish, "silver"), and Rio Grande.

Colorado College founded at Colorado Springs; University of Colorado, originally authorized by first territorial legislature, established with fund of $15,000 on condition that city of Boulder match the amount. |
| 1875 | *March 3.* Congress passed new enabling act authorizing territory to call another constitutional convention preparatory to admission to Union. |

December 20. Constitutional convention met in Denver.

Lead carbonate ores, rich in silver, discovered near site of present-day Leadville. Within two years, the vastness of the silver lodes made Leadville the richest mining center in the world.

1876   *January 31.* San Juan county created.

July 1. New constitution was approved by voters.

August 1. President U.S. Grant formally proclaimed Colorado's admission to Union as the "Centennial State." John L. Routt, last territorial governor, was elected first state governor. United States Senators were Henry M. Teller, early territorial lawyer, and Jerome B. Chafee, one of founders of city of Denver.

1877   *January 18.* Uncompahgre (later Ouray) county created.

January 29. <u>Routt</u> county, named for governor, created.

March 9. Custer county (named for <u>General George Custer</u>) and Gunnison county (named for <u>John W. Gunnison</u>) created.

University of Colorado opened its doors at Boulder.

1878   Central City opened its opera house. During the height of the community's prosperity, some of the leading actors and singers of the country performed there.

1879   First telephone exchange opened in Denver.

Nathan C. Meeker and several employees at Ute Indian agency were massacred; tribe was rounded up and resettled on reservation in southwestern Colorado.

February 10. Lake county renamed for Senator Chaffee; Carbonate County renamed Lake county.

1880 Census showed population of 194,327, nearly fivefold increase in decade.

Colorado supreme court heard suit between two railroads seeking right of way through Royal Gorge, and found in favor of Denver & Rio Grande Railroad.

1881 Grand Junction founded, at junction of Colorado and Gunnison rivers.

February 19. Dolores county established (Spanish for "sorrows," for El Rio de Nuestra Senor de los Dolores).

February 23. Pitkin county founded; named for Frederick W. Pitkin, second governor of Colorado.

1882 First steel to be milled from Colorado turned out at Pueblo.

1883 *February 10.* Garfield county created, named for President James A. Garfield.

February 11. Delta, Eagle, and Montrose counties formed; latter was named for Sir Walter Scott's novel, *The Legend of Montrose*.

February 14. Mesa county established (Spanish, "table").

1885	*April 14.* Archuleta county formed; named for Antonio D. Archuleta, state senator.
1886	Denver Union Stockyards, country's largest market for sheep, was established.
1887	*February 9.* Washington county, named for first President, created.
	February 25. Logan county established; named for Vice-President John A. Logan of Illinois.
1888	Ute Indians from Utah made final Indian raid in Colorado; they were soon rounded up and returned to reservation.
	Greeley, one of the most successful of the "colony towns," completed 900,000 acre irrigation project.
1889	*February 19.* Morgan, one of thirteen new counties to be created at this session of legislature, named for Christopher A. Morgan.
	March 15. Yuma county established.
	March 25. Cheyenne, Otero, and Rio Blanco counties established. Otero was named for Governor Miguel Otero of New Mexico.
	March 27. Phillips county named for R.O. Phillips, secretary of Lincoln Land Company.
	April 9. Sedgwick county named for John Sedgwick, Civil War officer killed at Spotsylvania.
	April 11. Kiowa, Kit Carson, Lincoln and Prowers counties established. First three named for Indian tribe, frontier scout and President, fourth for John W. Prowers, an early settler.

April 16. Baca and Montezuma counties named respectively for early pioneer family and for Aztec chief.

1890 Population: 413,249.

Sherman Silver Purchase Act passed by Congress, setting minimum price for buying of silver for public use and stimulating new prospecting. Large new fields were soon found on Rio Grande.

1891 Vast new gold field discovered at Cripple Creek.

Pike's Peak cog railway was formally opened.

White River Forest Reserve, first in Colorado, was opened.

1893 Repeal of Sherman Silver Purchase Act contributed to sudden collapse of economy in Colorado.

March 27. Mineral county established.

November 2. Colorado became second state to provide for woman suffrage.

1894 State capitol was completed, at cost of $2,500,000.

1898 *May 23.* Famous mining case of Del Monte Co. v. Last Chance Co. was decided by Supreme Court; holding among other things that a vein of ore whose apex falls within the bounds of one claim may be pursued to any depth beyond claim.

1899 *March 23.* Teller county named for <u>Henry M. Teller</u>, United States Senator and Secretary of Interior under President <u>Chester A. Arthur</u>.

CHRONOLOGY

1900   Population: 539,700.

Gold production reached record annual peak of $20,000,000.

1901   *March 18.* Denver county established.

April 15. Adams county named for <u>Alva Adams</u>, three-time governor of Colorado.

1902   Beet sugar refinery opened at Fort Collins, launching new agricultural industry.

1903   Two-year series of strikes began in mines, with frequent violence at Cripple Creek. Colorado national guard was activated to restore order.

1906   Mesa Verde National Park created by act of Congress.

1907   Denver Juvenile Court was opened under Judge <u>Ben B. Lindsey</u>. In time its new departures in administration of justice for minors would make it a model throughout the world.

1909   *May 5.* Jackson county, named for President <u>Andrew Jackson</u>, established.

1910   Population: 799,124.

1911   After extended litigation, Denver city and county were permitted to merge, one of the first instances of metropolitan area becoming coterminous with county.

February 27. Moffat county named for railroad magnate <u>David H. Moffat</u>.

May 29. Crowley county named for <u>John H. Crowley</u>, state political leader.

Colorado adopted primary election law.

1913	Constitutional amendment provided for jury service by women.
	March 8. Alamaso County created (Spanish for "cottonwood grove").
	April 20. "Battle of Ludlow" near Trinidad resulted in deaths of several women and children during prolonged series of strikes in coal mines.
1915	Workmen's compensation law adopted and state industrial commission established.
	January 12. Rocky Mountain National Park established.
1920	Population: 939,629.
1921	Devastating flood in Pueblo; $20,000,000 in losses.
1922	Moffat Tunnel, a bore of more than six miles under Continental Divide, was undertaken through special legislative act.
1927	Moffat Tunnel was completed at cost of $18,000,000. At the time it was considered one of engineering marvels of the world.
	Helium gas deposits were discovered near Thatcher.
1930	Population: 1,035,791.
1937	Colorado-Big Thompson project, more than 13 miles across Continental Divide to bring western water to northeastern irrigation area, authorized by Congress.
	Old age pensions, $45 monthly, most liberal in nation, went into effect; provided by constitutional amendment in 1936.

CHRONOLOGY 15

1940 Population: 1,123,296.

1947 Major legislative program undertaken for schools; $2,150,000 as county tax replacement, $6,000,000 in general state support.

1949 Colorado and Arkansas River compacts with neighboring states ratified, making possible coordinated conservation and use planning.

1950 Population: 1,325,089.

1953 *July 1.* Drought-stricken parts of state declared disaster area by President Eisenhower.

1954 *June 24.* Site near Colorado Springs selected for Air Force Academy.

September 9. Laboratory of solar physics dedicated at University of Colorado High Altitude Observatory near Climax.

1956 *August 11.* Final irrigation branches of Colorado-Big Thompson project completed.

1957 Union Oil Company opened $7,000,000 prototype retort to recover oil from shale deposits, near Grand Junction.

Uranium prospecting near Montrose touched off one of greatest land rushes since days of gold strikes.

1958 *August 29.* First class entered new Air Force Academy, $133,500,000 construction.

1960 Population: 1,753,947.

1961 *November.* Police corruption scandal in Denver prompted drafting of comprehensive plan for reform and modernization.

1962	*May 29.* Lt. Comdr. <u>Scott Carpenter</u> feted in hometown of Boulder for first American space flight in orbit around earth.

Congress approved $70,000,000 Frying Pan-Arkansas River project to bring western water to southeastern irrigation area. |
1967	*April 25.* Amid much controversy, legislature passed what was then nation's most liberal abortion law.
1969	*September 10.* Nuclear device detonated 8,000 feet underground to release quantities of natural gas trapped in compacted rock formations.
1970	Population: 2,207,259.
1971	*April 18.* White House Conference on Youth held at Estes Park.

The following list includes names of governors, United States Senators and United States Representatives from this state, for whom complete biographical data has been found. Names of persons living at the time of preparation of this list are usually omitted.

COLORADO

ADAMS, Alva B.
   b. Del Norte, Colo., Oct. 29, 1875
   d. Washington, D.C., Dec. 1, 1941
   U.S. Senator, 1923-24, 1933-41
   Governor, 1887-89, 1897-99, 1905
ADAMS, William H.
   b. Blue Mounds, Wis., Feb. 15, 1862
   d. Feb., 4, 1954
   Governor, 1927-33
AMMONS, Elias
   b. Mason Co., N.C., July 28, 1860
   d. May 20, 1925
   Governor, 1912-15
BELFORD, James B.
   b. Lewistown, Pa., Sept. 28, 1837
   d. Denver, Colo., Jan. 10, 1910
   U.S. Representative, 1876-77, 1877, 1879-85
BELL, John C.
   b. Sewanee, Tenn., Dec. 11, 1851
   d. Montrose, Colo., Aug. 12, 1933
   U.S. Representative, 1893-1903
BONYNGE, Robert W.
   b. New York City, N.Y., Sept. 8, 1863
   d. New York City, N.Y., Sept. 22, 1939
   U.S. Representative, 1904-09
BOWEN, Thomas M.
   b. Burlington, Iowa, Oct. 26, 1835
   d. Pueblo, Colo., Dec. 30, 1906
   U.S. Senator, 1883-89
   Governor of Idaho Territory, 1871
BROOKS, Franklin E.
   b. Sturbridge, Mass., Nov. 19, 1860
   d. St. Augustine, Fla., Feb. 7, 1916
   U.S. Representative, 1903-07

BUCHTEL, Henry A.
   b. Akron, Ohio, Sept. 30, 1847
   d. Oct. 22, 1924
   Governor, 1907-09
CARLSON, George A.
   b. Buena Vista Co., Iowa, Oct. 23, 1876
   d. Dec. 6, 1926
   Governor, 1915-17
CARR, Ralph
   b. Rosita, Colo., Dec. 11, 1887
   d. Sept. 22, 1950
   Governor, 1939-43
CHAFFEE, Jerome B.
   b. Niagara Co., N.Y., April 17, 1825
   d. Salem Center, N.Y., March 9, 1886
   U.S. Senator, 1876-79
CHILCOTT, George M.
   b. Cassville, Pa., Jan. 2, 1828
   d. St. Louis, Mo., March 6, 1891
   U.S. Senator, 1882-83
COOK, George W.
   b. Bedford, Ind., Nov. 10, 1851
   d. Pueblo, Colo., Dec. 18, 1916
   U.S. Representative, 1907-09
COOPER, Job A.
   b. Bond Co., Ill., Nov. 6, 1843
   d. 1899
   Governor, 1889-91
COSTIGAN, Edward P.
   b. King William Co., Va., July 1, 1874
   d. Denver, Colo., Jan. 17, 1939
   U.S. Senator, 1931-37
CUMMINGS, Fred
   b. Groveton, N.H., Sept. 18, 1864
   d. Ft. Collins, Colo., Nov. 10, 1952
   U.S. Representative, 1933-41
EATON, Benjamin H.
   b. Zanesville, Ohio, Dec. 15, 1833
   d. Oct. 29, 1886
   Governor, 1885-86
EATON, William R.
   b. Nova Scotia, Can., Dec. 17, 1877
   d. Denver, Colo., Dec. 16, 1942
   U.S. Representative, 1929-33

GRANT, James B.
    b. Russell Co., Ala., Jan. 2, 1848
    d. Nov. 1, 1911
    Governor, 1883-85

GUGGENHEIM, Simon
    b. Philadelphia, Pa., Dec. 30, 1867
    d. New York City, N.Y., Nov. 2, 1941
    U.S. Senator, 1907-13

GUNTER, Julius C.
    b. Fayetteville, Ark., Oct. 31, 1858
    d. Oct. 26, 1940
    Governor, 1917-19

HAGGOTT, Warren A.
    b. Sidney, Ohio, May 18, 1864
    d. Denver, Colo., April 29, 1958
    U.S. Representative, 1907-09

HARDY, Guy U.
    b. Abingdon, Ill., April 4, 1872
    d. Canon City, Colo., Jan. 26, 1947
    U.S. Representative, 1919-33

HILL, Nathaniel P.
    b. Montgomery, N.Y., Feb. 18, 1832
    d. Denver, Colo., May 22, 1900
    U.S. Senator, 1879-85

HILLIARD, Benjamin C.
    b. Osceola, Iowa, Jan. 9, 1868
    d. Denver, Colo., Aug. 7, 1951
    U.S. Representative, 1915-19

HOGG, Herschel M.
    b. Youngstown, Ohio, Nov. 21, 1853
    d. Denver, Colo., Aug. 27, 1934
    U.S. Representative, 1903-07

HUGHES, Charles J. Jr.
    b. Kingston, Mo., Feb. 16, 1853
    d. Denver, Colo., Jan. 11, 1911
    U.S. Senator, 1904-11

KINDEL, George J.
    b. Cincinnati, Ohio, March 2, 1855
    d. Brush, Colo., Feb. 28, 1930
    U.S. Representative, 1913-15

KNOUS, W. Lee
    b. Ouray, Colo., Feb. 2, 1889
    d. Dec., 1959
    Governor, 1947-50

LEWIS, Lawrence
    b. St. Louis, Mo., June 22, 1879
    d. Washington, D.C., Dec. 9, 1943
    U.S. Representative, 1933-43
MARTIN, John A.
    b. Cincinnati, Ohio, April 10, 1868
    d. Washington, D.C., Dec. 23, 1939
    U.S. Representative, 1909-13
MCDONALD, Jesse
    b. Ashtabula, Ohio, June 30, 1858
    d. Feb. 24, 1942
    Governor, 1905-06
MEANS, Rice W.
    b. St. Joseph, Mo., Nov. 16, 1877
    d. Denver, Colo., Jan. 30, 1949
    U.S. Senator, 1924-27
MILLIKIN, Eugene D.
    b. Hamilton, Ohio, Feb. 12, 1891
    d. Denver, Colo., July 26, 1958
    U.S. Senator, 1941-57
NICHOLSON, Samuel D.
    b. Springfield, P.E. Island, Can., Feb. 22, 1859
    d. Denver, Colo., March 24, 1923
    U.S. Senator, 1921-23
PATTERSON, Thomas M.
    b. County Carlow, Ireland, Nov. 4, 1839
    d. Denver, Colo., July 23, 1916
    U.S. Representative, 1877-79
    U.S. Senator, 1901-07
PEABODY, James H.
    b. Topsham, Vt., Aug. 21, 1852
    d. Nov. 23, 1917
    Governor, 1902-05
PENCE, Lafayette
    b. Columbus, Ind., Dec. 23, 1857
    d. Washington, D.C., Oct. 22, 1923
    U.S. Representative, 1893-95
PHIPPS, Lawrence C.
    b. Amwell Township, Pa., Aug. 30, 1862
    d. Santa Monica, Cal., March 1, 1958
    U.S. Senator, 1919-31

PITKIN, Frederick
    b. Manchester, Conn., Aug. 31, 1837
    d. Pueblo, Colo., Dec. 18, 1886
    Governor, 1878-83
ROCKWELL, Robert F.
    b. Cortland, N.Y., Feb. 11, 1886
    d. Maher, Colo., Sept. 29, 1950
    U.S. Representative, 1941-49
ROUTT, John L.
    b. Eddyville, Colo., April 25, 1826
    d. 1907
    Governor, 1875-76, 1876-78, 1890-92
RUCKER, Atterson W.
    b. Harrodsburg, Ky., April 3, 1847
    d. Mt. Morrison, Colo., July 19, 1924
    U.S. Representative, 1909-13
SCHUYLER, Karl C.
    b. Colorado Springs, Colo., April 3, 1877
    d. New York City, N.Y., July 31, 1933
    U.S. Senator, 1932-33
SELDOMRIDGE, Harry H.
    b. Philadelphia, Pa., Oct. 1, 1864
    d. Colorado Springs, Colo., Nov. 2, 1927
    U.S. Representative, 1913-15
SHAFROTH, John F.
    b. Fayette, Mo., June 9, 1854
    d. Denver, Colo., Feb. 20, 1922
    U.S. Representative, 1895-1904
    U.S. Senator, 1913-19
    Governor, 1908-12
SHOUP, Oliver H.
    b. Champaign Co., Ill., Dec. 13, 1869
    d. Sept. 30, 1940
    Governor, 1919-23
SWEET, William E.
    b. Chicago, Ill., Jan. 27, 1869
    d. May 9, 1942
    Governor, 1923-24
SYMES, George G.
    b. Ashtabula Co., Ohio, April 28, 1840
    d. Denver, Colo., Nov. 3, 1893
    U.S. Representative, 1885-89

TABOR, Horace A.W.
   b. Holland, Vt., Nov. 26, 1830
   d. Denver, Colo., April 10, 1899
   U.S. Senator, 1883

TAYLOR, Edward T.
   b. Metamora, Ill., June 19, 1858
   d. Denver, Colo., Sept. 3, 1941
   U.S. Representative, 1909-41

TELLER, Henry M.
   b. Granger, N.Y., May 23, 1830
   d. Denver, Colo., Feb. 23, 1914
   U.S. Senator, 1876-82, 1885-1909
   Sec. of Interior, 1882-85

THOMAS, Charles S.
   b. Darien, Ga., Dec. 6, 1849
   d. Denver, Colo., June 24, 1934
   U.S. Senator, 1913-21
   Governor, 1899-1901

TIMBERLAKE, Charles B.
   b. Wilmington, Ohio, Sept. 25, 1854
   d. Sterling, Colo., May 31, 1941
   U.S. Representative, 1915-33

TOWNSEND, Hosea
   b. Greenwich, Ohio, June 16, 1840
   d. Ardmore, Okla., March 4, 1909
   U.S. Representative, 1889-93

VAILE, William N.
   b. Kokomo, Ind., June 22, 1876
   d. Rocky Mtn. Nat'l Park, Colo., July 2, 1927
   U.S. Representative, 1919-27

VIVIAN, John C.
   b. Golden, Colo., June 30, 1887
   d. Dec. 10, 1964
   Governor, 1843-47

WAITE, Davis H.
   b. Jamestown, N.Y., April 9, 1825
   d. 1901
   Governor, 1893-94

WALKER, Walter
   b. Marion, Ky., April 3, 1883
   d. Grand Junction, Colo., Oct. 8, 1956
   U.S. Senator, 1932

WATERMAN, Charles W.
    b. Waitsfield, Vt., Nov. 2, 1861
    d. Washington, D.C., Aug. 27, 1932
    U.S. Senator, 1927-32
WHITE, S. Harrison
    b. Maries Co., Mo., Dec. 24, 1864
    d. Colorado Springs, Colo., Dec. 21, 1945
    U.S. Representative, 1927-29
WOLCOTT, Edward O.
    b. Long Meadow, Mass., March 26, 1848
    d. Monte Carlo, Monaco, March 1, 1905
    U.S. Senator, 1889-1901

OUTLINE OF CONSTITUTION

Preamble
Article I.   Boundaries
Article II.   Bill of Rights (§§ 1-28)
Article III.   Distribution of Powers
Article IV.   Executive Department (§§ 1-21)
Article V.   Legislative Department (§§ 1-47)
Article VI.   Judicial Department (§§ 1-31)
Article VII.   Suffrage and Elections (§§ 1-12)
Article VIII.   State Institutions (§§ 1-5)
Article IX.   Education (§§ 1-16)
Article X.   Revenue (§§ 1-18)
Article XI.   Public Indebtedness (§§ 1-9)
Article XII.   Officers (§§ 1-14)
Article XIII.   Impeachments (§§ 1-3)
Article XIV.   Counties (§§ 1-15)
Article XV.   Corporations (§§ 1-15)
Article XVI.   Mining and Irrigation (§§1-8)
Article XVII.   Militia (§§ 1-5)
Article XVIII.   Miscellaneous (§§ 1-8)
Article XIX.   Amendments (§§ 1-2)
Article XX.   City and County of Denver and Other Home Rule Cities and Towns (§§ 1-8)
Article XXI.   Recall from Office (§§ 1-4)
Article XXII.   Intoxicating Liquors (§ 1)
Article XXIII.   Publication of Legal Advertising (§ 1)
Article XXIV.   Old Age Pensions (§§ 1-9)
Article XXV.   Public Utilities
Schedule (§§ 1-22)

PREAMBLE

ARTICLE I. BOUNDARIES

ARTICLE II. BILL OF RIGHTS

Sec. 1. Vestment of political power
Sec. 2. People may alter or abolish form of government; proviso
Sec. 3. Inalienable rights
Sec. 4. Religious freedom
Sec. 5. Freedom of elections
Sec. 6. Equality of justice
Sec. 7. Security of person and property; searches; seizures; warrants
Sec. 8. Prosecutions; indictment or information
Sec. 9. Treason; estates of suicides
Sec. 10. Freedom of speech and press
Sec. 11. Ex post facto laws
Sec. 12. No imprisonment for debt
Sec. 13. Right to bear arms
Sec. 14. Taking private property for private use
Sec. 15. Taking property for public use; compensation, how ascertained
Sec. 16. Criminal prosecutions; rights of defendant
Sec. 17. Imprisonment of witnesses; depositions; form
Sec. 18. Crimes; evidence against one's self; jeopardy
Sec. 19. Right to bail
Sec. 20. Excessive bail, fines or punishment
Sec. 21. Suspension of habeas corpus
Sec. 22. Military subject to civil power; quartering of troops
Sec. 23. Trial by jury; grand jury
Sec. 24. Right to assemble and petition
Sec 25. Due process of law
Sec. 26. Slavery prohibited
Sec. 27. Property rights of aliens
Sec. 28. Rights reserved not disparaged

ARTICLE III. DISTRIBUTION OF POWERS

ARTICLE IV. EXECUTIVE DEPARTMENT
Sec. 1. Officers; terms of office; residence
Sec. 2. Governor supreme executive
Sec. 3. State officers; election; returns
Sec. 4. Qualifications of state officers
Sec. 5. Governor commander-in-chief of militia
Sec. 6. Appointment of officers; vacancy
Sec. 7. Governor may grant reprieves and pardons
Sec. 8. Governor may require information from officers; message
Sec. 9. Governor may convene legislature or senate
Sec. 10. Governor may adjourn legislature
Sec. 11. Bills presented to governor; veto; return
Sec. 12. Governor may veto items in appropriation bills; reconsideration
Sec. 13. Lieutenant-governor acts as governor; when
Sec. 14. Lieutenant-governor president of senate; president pro tem
Sec. 15. No lieutenant-governor; who to act as governor
Sec. 16. Account and report of moneys
Sec. 17. Executive officers to make report
Sec. 18. State seal
Sec. 19. Salaries of officers; fees paid into treasury
Sec. 20. State librarian
Sec. 21. Auditor and treasurer ineligible for re-election

ARTICLE V. LEGISLATIVE DEPARTMENT
Sec. 1. General assembly; initiative and referendum
Sec. 2. Election of members; vacancies
Sec. 3. Terms of senators and representatives
Sec. 4. Qualifications of members
Sec. 5. Classification of senators
Sec. 6. Compensation of members
Sec. 7. General assembly; shall meet when; term of members; committees
Sec 8. Members precluded from holding office
Sec. 9. Increase of salary; when forbidden
Sec. 10. Each house to choose its officers
Sec. 11. Quorum
Sec. 12. Each house makes and enforces rules
Sec. 13. Journal; ayes and nays to be entered, when
Sec. 14. Open sessions
Sec. 15. Adjournment for more than three days
Sec. 16. Privileges of members
Sec. 17. No law passed but by bill; amendments
Sec. 18. Enacting clause
Sec. 19. When laws take effect; introduction of bills
Sec. 20. Bills referred to committee; printed
Sec. 21. Bill to contain but one subject; expressed in title
Sec. 22. Reading and passage of bills
Sec. 23. Vote on amendments and report of committee
Sec. 24. Revival, amendment or extension of laws
Sec. 25. Special legislation prohibited
Sec. 25a. Eight hour employment
Sec. 26. Signing of bills
Sec. 27. Officers and employees; compensation
Sec. 28. Extra compensation to officers, employees or contractors forbidden
Sec. 29. Contracts for quarters, furnishings and supplies
Sec. 30. Salary of governor and judges to be fixed by legislature; term not to be extended or salaries increased or decreased
Sec. 31. Revenue bills
Sec. 32. Appropriation bills
Sec. 33. Disbursement of public money
Sec. 34. Appropriations to private institutions forbidden
Sec. 35. Delegation of power
Sec. 36. Laws on investment of trust funds
Sec. 37. Change of venue
Sec. 38. No liability exchanged or released
Sec. 39. Orders and resolutions presented to governor
Sec. 40. Bribery and influence in general assembly
Sec. 41. Offering, giving, promising money or other consideration
Sec. 42. Corrupt solicitation of members and officers
Sec. 43. Member interested shall not vote

CONGRESSIONAL AND LEGISLATIVE APPORTIONMENTS
Sec. 44. Representatives in congress
Sec. 45. Census
Sec. 46. Number of members of general assembly
Sec. 47. Senatorial and representative districts

ARTICLE VI. JUDICIAL DEPARTMENT
Sec. 1. Vestment of judicial power

SUPREME COURT
Sec. 2. Appellate jurisdiction
Sec. 3. Original jurisdiction; opinions
Sec. 4. Terms
Sec. 5. Personnel of court; departments
Sec. 6. Election of judges
Sec. 7. Term of office
Sec. 8. Appointment and election of judges
Sec. 9. Clerk of supreme court
Sec. 10. Qualifications of judges

DISTRICT COURTS
Sec. 11. Jurisdiction
Sec. 12. Judicial districts; term of judges
Sec. 13. Judicial districts
Sec 14. Number of districts increased or diminished

OUTLINE OF CONSTITUTION

Sec. 15. Election of judges; term
Sec. 16. Qualifications of district judges
Sec. 17. Terms of court
Sec. 18. Compensation and services of judges
Sec. 19. Clerk of district court
Sec. 20. Judges may fix terms, when

DISTRICT ATTORNEY
Sec. 21. Election; term; salary; qualifications

COUNTY COURTS
Sec. 22. Judge; election; term; salary
Sec. 23. Court of record; jurisdiction; appeals; writs of error

CONCURRENT CRIMINAL COURT
Sec. 24. In what counties; jurisdiction

JUSTICES OF THE PEACE
Sec. 25. Jurisdiction

POLICE MAGISTRATES
Sec. 26. How created; jurisdiction

MISCELLANEOUS
Sec. 27. Judges to report defects in laws; governor to transmit
Sec. 28. Laws relating to courts; uniform
Sec. 29. Where officers must reside; vacancies
Sec. 30. Process; run in name of people
Sec. 31. Retirement of judges

ARTICLE VII. SUFFRAGE AND ELECTIONS
Sec. 1. Qualifications of elector
Sec. 2. Suffrage to women
Sec. 3. Educational qualifications of elector
Sec. 4. When residence does not change
Sec. 5. Privilege of voters
Sec. 6. Electors only eligible to office
Sec. 7. General election
Sec. 8. Elections by ballot or voting machine
Sec. 9. No privilege to witness in election trial
Sec. 10. Disfranchisement during imprisonment
Sec. 11. Purity of elections
Sec. 12. Election contests; by whom tried

ARTICLE VIII. STATE INSTITUTIONS
Sec. 1. Established and supported by state
Sec. 2. Seat of government; how located
Sec. 3. Seat of government; how changed
Sec. 4. Appropriation for capitol building
Sec. 5. Educational institutions

ARTICLE IX. EDUCATION
Sec. 1. Supervision of schools; board of education
Sec. 2. Establishment and maintenance of public schools
Sec. 3. School fund inviolate
Sec. 4. County treasurer to collect and disburse
Sec. 5. Of what school fund consists
Sec. 6. County superintendent of schools
Sec. 7. Aid to private schools, churches, sectarian purpose, forbidden
Sec. 8. Religious test and race discrimination forbidden; sectarian tenets
Sec. 9. State board of land commissioners
Sec. 10. Selection and control of public lands
Sec. 11. Compulsory education
Sec. 12. Regents of university
Sec. 13. President of university
Sec. 14. Control of university
Sec. 15. School districts; board of education
Sec. 16. Text books in public schools

ARTICLE X. REVENUE
Sec. 1. Fiscal year
Sec. 2. Tax provided for state expenses
Sec. 3. Uniform taxation; exemptions
Sec. 4. Public property exempt
Sec. 5. Property used for religious worship, schools and charitable purposes exempt
Sec. 6. Other exemptions void; specific ownership tax on motor vehicles
Sec. 7. Municipal taxation by general assembly prohibited
Sec. 8. No county, city, town to be released
Sec. 9. Relinquishment of power to tax corporations forbidden
Sec. 10. Corporations subject to tax
Sec. 11. Maximum rate of taxation
Sec. 12. Report of state treasurer
Sec. 13. Making profit on public money; felony
Sec. 14. Private property not taken for public debt
Sec. 15. Boards of equalization; duties
Sec. 16. Appropriations not to exceed tax; exceptions
Sec. 17. Income tax
Sec. 18. License fees and excise taxes; use of

ARTICLE XI. PUBLIC INDEBTEDNESS
Sec. 1. Pledging credit of state, county, city, town or school district forbidden
Sec. 2. No aid to corporations; no joint ownership by state, county, city, town or school district
Sec. 3. Public debt of state; limitations
Sec. 4. Law creating debt
Sec. 5. Debt for public buildings; how created
Sec. 6. County indebtedness; how created; limit; refunding
Sec. 7. Debt for school buildings; how created
Sec. 8. City indebtedness; ordinance, tax, water obligations excepted
Sec. 9. This article not to affect prior obligations

ARTICLE XII. OFFICERS
Sec. 1. When office expires; suspension by law
Sec. 2. Personal attention required

Sec. 3. Defaulting collector disqualified from office
Sec. 4. Disqualifications from holding office of trust or profit
Sec. 5. Investigation of state and county treasurers
Sec. 6. Bribery of officers defined
Sec. 7. Oath of members of general assembly
Sec. 8. Oath of civil officers
Sec. 9. Oaths; where filed
Sec. 10. Refusal to qualify; vacancy
Sec. 11. Vacancy; term of officer elected to fill
Sec. 12. Duel; disqualifies for office
Sec. 13. Civil service; apply merit system
Sec. 14. Veterans preference

ARTICLE XIII. IMPEACHMENTS
Sec. 1. House impeach; senate try; conviction; when chief justice presides
Sec. 2. Who liable to impeachment; judgment; no bar to prosecution
Sec. 3. Officers not subject to impeachment subject to removal

ARTICLE XIV. COUNTIES
Sec. 1. Counties of state
Sec. 2. Removal of county seats
Sec. 3. Striking off territory; vote
Sec. 4. New county shall pay proportion of debt
Sec. 5. Part stricken off; pay proportion of debt

COUNTY OFFICERS
Sec. 6. County commissioners; election; term
Sec. 7. Officers' compensation
Sec. 8. County officers; election; term; salary
Sec. 9. Vacancies; how filled
Sec. 10. Elector only eligible to county office
Sec. 11. Justices of the peace; constables
Sec. 12. Other officers
Sec. 13. Classification of cities and towns
Sec. 14. Existing cities and towns may come under general law
Sec. 15. Classifying counties as to fees

ARTICLE XV. CORPORATIONS
Sec. 1. Unused charters or grants of privilege
Sec. 2. Corporate charters created by general law
Sec. 3. Power to revoke, alter or annul charter
Sec. 4. Railroads; common carriers; construction; intersection
Sec. 5. Consolidation of parallel lines forbidden
Sec. 6. Equal rights of public to transportation
Sec. 7. Existing railroads to file acceptance of constitution
Sec. 8. Eminent domain; police power; not to be abridged

Sec. 9. Fictitious stock, bonds; increase of stock
Sec. 10. Foreign corporations; place; agent
Sec. 11. Street railroads; consent of municipality
Sec. 12. Retrospective laws not to be passed
Sec. 13. Telegraph lines; consolidation
Sec. 14. Railroad or telegraph companies; consolidating with foreign companies
Sec. 15. Contracts with employees releasing from liability; void

ARTICLE XVI. MINING AND IRRIGATION
MINING
Sec. 1. Commissioner of mines
Sec. 2. Ventilation; employment of children
Sec. 3. Drainage
Sec. 4. Mining, metallurgy, in public institutions

IRRIGATION
Sec. 5. Water of streams public property
Sec. 6. Diverting unappropriated water; priority preferred uses
Sec. 7. Right of way for ditches, flumes
Sec. 8. County commissioners to fix rates for water, when

ARTICLE XVII. MILITIA
Sec. 1. Persons subject to service
Sec. 2. Organization; equipment; discipline
Sec. 3. Officers; how chosen
Sec. 4. Armories
Sec. 5. Exemption in time of peace

ARTICLE XVIII. MISCELLANEOUS
Sec. 1. Homestead and exemption laws
Sec. 2. Lotteries
Sec. 3. Arbitration laws
Sec. 4. Felony defined
Sec. 5. Spurious and d r u g g e d liquors; laws concerning
Sec. 6. Preservation of forests
Sec. 7. Land value increase; arboreal planting exempt
Sec. 8. Publication of laws

ARTICLE XIX. AMENDMENTS
Sec. 1. Constitutional convention; h o w called
Sec. 2. Amendments to constitution; how adopted

ARTICLE XX. CITY AND COUNTY OF DENVER AND OTHER HOME RULE CITIES AND TOWNS
Sec. 1. Incorporated
Sec. 2. Officers
Sec. 3. Transfer of government
Sec. 4. First charter
Sec. 5. New c h a r t e r s, amendments or measures
Sec. 6. Home rule for cities and towns
Sec. 7. City and county of Denver single school district; consolidations

OUTLINE OF CONSTITUTION

Sec. 8. Conflicting constitutional provisions declared inapplicable

ARTICLE XXI. RECALL FROM OFFICE
Sec. 1. State officers may be recalled
Sec. 2. Form of recall petition
Sec. 3. Resignation; filling vacancy
Sec. 4. Recall of officers

ARTICLE XXII. INTOXICATING LIQUORS
Sec 1. Repeal of intoxicating liquor laws

ARTICLE XXIII. PUBLICATION OF LEGAL ADVERTISING
Sec. 1. Publication of proposed constitutional amendments and initiated and referred bills

ARTICLE XXIV. OLD AGE PENSIONS
Sec. 1. Fund created
Sec. 2. Moneys allocated to fund
Sec. 3. Persons entitled to receive pensions
Sec. 4. The state board of public welfare to administer fund
Sec. 5. Revenues for old age pension fund continued
Sec. 6. Basic minimum award
Sec. 7. Stabilization fund and health and medical care fund
Sec. 8. Fund to remain inviolate
Sec. 9. Effective date

ARTICLE XXV. PUBLIC UTILITIES

SCHEDULE
Sec. 1. All laws remain till repealed
Sec. 2. Contracts; recognizances; indictments
Sec. 3. Territorial property vests in state
Sec. 4. Duty of general assembly
Sec. 5. Supreme and district courts; transition
Sec. 6. Judges; district attorneys; terms commence on filing oath
Sec. 7. Seals of supreme and district courts
Sec. 8. Probate court; county court
Sec. 9. Terms probate court, probate judge, apply to county court, county judge
Sec. 10. County and precinct officers
Sec. 11. Vacancies in county offices
Sec. 12. Constitution takes effect on president's proclamation
Sec. 13. First election, contest
Sec. 14. First election; canvass
Sec. 15. Senators; representatives; districts
Sec. 16. Congressional election; canvass
Sec. 17. General assembly, first session; restrictions removed
Sec. 18. First general election; canvass
Sec. 19. Presidential electors, 1876
Sec. 20. Presidential electors after 1876
Sec. 21. Expenses of convention
Sec. 22. Recognizances, bonds, payable to people continue

SELECTED DOCUMENTS

Samuel Bowles, famed editor of the Springfield (Mass.) *Republican,* called Colorado and the Rockies "the Switzerland of America," and certainly the travelers of the late nineteenth century found both the new cities and the surrounding scenic countryside thoroughly captivating. Isabella L. Bird was one such traveller who came to Colorado a few years after it had become a state, and who wrote a series of letters to her sister describing her experiences in the frontier mountain region. She then gathered the letters into book form and published them under the title, *A Lady's Life in the Rocky Mountains* (New York, 1880).

Another traveler, a decade and a half later, was especially interested in the rapidly growing community of Denver, which Julian Ralph described in an article in *Harper's Magazine* for May, 1893.

Colorado had its share of both political progress and political corruption at the turn of the century, and the single individual who caught the national fancy and dramatized the crusade for improvement was Judge Ben B. Lindsey, controversial leader of reform movements of many types but unquestioned leader in reform of juvenile justice. The Denver Juvenile Court under his administration attracted attention from social workers and jurists throughout the world. His flamboyant struggles with machine politicians in order to get an adequate juvenile court program is part of a series of articles about "The Beast," which he wrote in collaboration with Harvey J. O'Higgins of *Everybody's Magazine,* which published the articles in 1909-10.

A LADY'S LIFE IN THE ROCKY MOUNTAINS
by
Isabella L. Bird

LETTER VIII.

Estes Park — Big Game — "Parks" in Colorado — **Magnificent** Scenery — Flowers and Pines — An awful Road — Our Log Cabin — Griffith Evans — A miniature World — Our Topics — A night Alarm — A Skunk — Morning glories — Daily routine — The Panic "Wait for the Waggon" — A musical evening.

ESTES PARK, COLORADO TERRITORY, *October 2.*

How time has slipped by I do not know. This is a glorious region, and the air and life are intoxicating. I live mainly out of doors and on horseback, wear my half threadbare Hawaiian dress, sleep sometimes under the stars on a bed of pine boughs, ride on a Mexican saddle, and hear once more the low music of my Mexican spurs. "There's a stranger! Heave arf a brick at him!" is said by many travellers to express the feeling of the new settlers in these Territories. This is not my experience in my cheery mountain home. How the rafters ring as I write with songs and mirth, while the pitch-pine logs blaze and crackle in the chimney, and the fine snow-dust drives in through the chinks and forms mimic snow-wreaths on the floor, and the wind raves and howls and plays among the creaking pine branches and snaps them short off, and the lightning plays round the blasted top of Long's Peak, and the hardy hunters divert themselves with the thought that when I go to bed I must turn out and face the storm!

You will ask, "What is Estes Park?" This name, with the quiet Midland Counties' sound, suggests "park palings" well lichened, a lodge with a curtseying woman, fallow-deer, and a Queen Anne mansion. Such as it is, Estes Park is mine. It is unsurveyed, "no man's land," and mine by right of love, appropriation, and appreciation; by the seizure of its peerless sunrises and sunsets, its glorious afterglow, its blazing noons, its hurricanes sharp and furious, its wild auroras, its glories of mountain and forest, of canyon, lake, and river, and the stereotyping them all in my memory. Mine, too, in a better than the sportsman's sense, are its majestic wapiti, which play and fight under the pines in the early morning, as securely as fallow-deer under our English oaks; its graceful "black-tails," swift of foot; its superb big-horns, whose noble leader is to be seen now and then with his classic head against the blue sky on the top of a colossal rock; its sneaking mountain lion with his hideous nocturnal caterwaulings, the great 'grizzly," the beautiful skunk, the wary beaver, who is always making lakes, damming and turning streams, cutting down young cotton-woods, and setting an example of thrift and industry; the wolf, greedy and

MY HOME IN THE ROCKY MOUNTAINS.

cowardly; the coyote and the lynx, and all the lesser fry of mink, marten, cat, hare, fox, squirrel, and chipmonk, as well as things that fly, from the eagle down to the crested blue-jay. May their number never be less, in spite of the hunter who kills for food and gain, and the sportsman who kills and marauds for pastime!

But still I have not answered the natural question,[1] "What is Estes Park?" Among the striking peculiarities of these mountains are hundreds of high-lying valleys, large and small, at heights varying from 6000 to 11,000 feet. The most important are North Park, held by hostile Indians; Middle Park, famous for hot springs and trout; South Park, rich in minerals; and San Luis Park. South Park is 10,000 feet high, a great rolling prairie 70 miles long, well grassed and watered, but nearly closed by snow in winter. But Parks innumerable are scattered throughout the mountains, most of them unnamed, and others nicknamed by the hunters or trappers who have made them their temporary resorts. They always lie far within the flaming Foot Hills, their exquisite stretches of flowery pastures dotted artistically with clumps of trees sloping lawnlike to bright swift streams full of red-

[1] Nor should I at this time, had not Henry Kingsley, Lord Dunraven, and "The Field," divulged the charms and whereabouts of these "happy hunting grounds," with the certain result of directing a stream of tourists into the solitary, beast-haunted paradise.

waistcoated trout, or running up in soft glades into the dark forest, above which the snow-peaks rise in their infinite majesty. Some are bits of meadow a mile long and very narrow, with a small stream, a beaver-dam, and a pond made by beaver industry. Hundreds of these can only be reached by riding in the bed of a stream, or by scrambling up some narrow canyon till it debouches on the fairy-like stretch above. These parks are the feeding-grounds of innumerable wild animals, and some, like one three miles off, seem chosen for the process of antler-casting, the grass being covered for at least a square mile with the magnificent branching horns of the elk.

Estes Park combines the beauties of all. Dismiss all thoughts of the Midland Counties. For park palings there are mountains, forest skirted, 9000, 11,000, 14,000 feet high; for a lodge, two sentinel peaks of granite guarding the only feasible entrance; and for a Queen Anne mansion an unchinked log cabin with a vault of sunny blue overhead. The park is most irregularly shaped, and contains hardly any level grass. It is an aggregate of lawns, slopes, and glades, about eighteen miles in length, but never more than two miles in width. The Big Thompson, a bright, rapid trout-stream, snow-born on Long's Peak a few miles higher, takes all sorts of magical twists, vanishing and reappearing unexpectedly, glancing among lawns, rushing through romantic ravines, everywhere making music through the still, long nights. Here and there the lawns are so smooth, the trees so artistically grouped, a lake makes such an artistic foreground, or a waterfall comes tumbling down with such an apparent feeling for the picturesque, that I am almost angry with Nature for her close imitation of art. But in another hundred yards Nature, glorious, unapproachable, inimitable, is herself again, raising one's thoughts reverently upwards to her Creator and ours. Grandeur and sublimity, not softness, are the features of Estes Park. The glades which begin so softly are soon lost in the dark primæval forests, with their peaks of rosy granite, and their stretches of granite blocks piled and poised by nature in some mood of fury. The streams are lost in canyons nearly or quite inaccessible, awful in their blackness and darkness; every valley ends in mystery; seven mountain ranges raise their frowning barriers between us and the Plains, and at the south end of the park Long's Peak rises to a height of 14,700 feet, with his bare, scathed head slashed with eternal snow. The lowest part of the Park is 7500 feet high; and though the sun is hot during the day, the mercury hovers near the freezing-point every night of the summer. An immense quantity of snow falls, but partly owing to the tremendous winds which drift it into the deep valleys, and partly to the bright warm sun of the winter months, the Park is never snowed up, and a number of cattle and horses are wintered out of doors on its sun-cured, saccharine grasses, of which the *gramma* grass is the most valuable. The soil here, as elsewhere in the neighbourhood, is nearly everywhere coarse, grey, granitic dust, produced probably by the disintegration of the surrounding mountains. It does not hold water, and is never wet in any weather. There are no thaws here. The snow mysteriously disappears by rapid evaporation. Oats grow, but do not ripen, and, when well advanced, are cut and stacked for winter fodder. Potatoes yield abundantly, and, though not very large, are of the best quality, mealy throughout. Evans has not attempted anything else, and probably the more succulent vegetables would require irrigation. The wild flowers are gorgeous and innumerable, though their beauty, which culminates in July and August, was over before I arrived, and the recent snow-flurries have finished them. The time between winter and winter is very short, and the flowery growth and blossom of a whole year are compressed into two months. Here are dandelions, buttercups, larkspurs, harebells, violets, roses, blue gentian, columbine, painter's brush, and fifty others, blue and yellow predominating; and though their blossoms are stiffened by the cold every morning, they are starring the grass and drooping over the brook long before noon, making the most of their brief lives in the sunshine. Of ferns, after many a long hunt, I have only found the *Cystopteris fragilis* and the *Blechnum spicant*, but I hear that the *Pteris aquilina* is also found. Snakes and mosquitoes do not appear to be known here. Coming almost direct from the tropics, one is dissatisfied with the uniformity of the foliage; indeed, foliage can hardly be written of, as the trees properly so called at this height are exclusively *Coniferæ*, and bear needles instead of leaves. In places there are patches of spindly aspens, which have turned a lemon-yellow, and along the streams bear-cherries, vines, and roses lighten the gulches with their variegated crimson leaves. The pines are not imposing, either from their girth or height. Their colouring is blackish-green, and though they are effective singly or in groups, they are sombre and almost funereal when densely massed, as here, along the mountain sides. The timber line is at a height of about 11,000 feet, and is singularly well defined. The most attractive tree I have seen is the silver spruce, *Abies Englemanii*, near of kin to what is often called the balsam-fir. Its shape and colour are both beautiful. My heart warms towards it, and I frequent all the places where I can find it. It looks as if a soft, blue, silver powder had fallen on its deep-green needles, or as if a bluish hoar-frost, which must melt at noon, were resting upon it. Anyhow, one can hardly believe that the beauty is permanent, and survives the summer heat and the winter cold. The universal tree here is the *Pinus ponderosa,* but it never attains any very considerable size, and there is nothing to compare with the red-woods of the Sierra Nevada, far less with the sequoias of California.

As I have written before, Estes Park is thirty miles from Longmount, the nearest settlement, and it can be reached on horseback only by the steep and devious track by which I came, passing through a narrow rift in the top of a precipitous ridge, 9000 feet high, called the Devil's Gate. Evans takes a lumber waggon with four horses over the mountains, and a Colorado engineer would have no difficulty in making a waggon road. In several of the gulches over which the track hangs there are the remains of waggons which have come to grief in the attempt to emulate Evans's feat, which, without evidence, I should have supposed to be impossible. It is an awful road. The only settlers in the Park are Griffith Evans, and a married man a mile higher up. "Mountain Jim's" cabin is in the entrance gulch, four miles off, and there is not another cabin for eighteen miles towards the Plains. The Park is unsurveyed, and the huge tract of mountainous country beyond is almost altogether unexplored. Elk-hunters occasionally come up and camp out here; but the two settlers, who, however, are only squatters, for various reasons are not disposed to encourage such visitors. When Evans, who is a very successful hunter, came here, he came on foot, and for some time after settling here he carried the flour and necessaries required by his family on his back over the mountains.

As I intend to make Estes Park my headquarters until the winter sets in, I must make you acquainted with my surroundings and mode of living. The "Queen Anne Mansion" is represented by a log cabin made of big hewn logs. The chinks should be filled with mud and lime, but these are wanting. The roof is formed of barked young spruce, then a layer of hay, and an outer coating of mud, all nearly flat. The floors are roughly boarded. The "living-room" is about sixteen feet square, and has a rough stone chimney in which pine logs are always burning. At one end there is a door into a small bedroom, and at the other a door into a small eating-room, at the table of which we feed in relays. This opens into a very small kitchen with a great American cooking-stove, and there are two "bed-closets" besides. Although rude, it is comfortable, except for the draughts. The fine snow drives in through the chinks and covers the floors, but sweeping it out at intervals is both fun and exercise. There are no heaps or rubbish-places outside. Near it, on the slope under the pines, is a pretty two-roomed cabin, and beyond that, near the lake, is my cabin, a very rough one. My door opens into a little room with a stone chimney, and that again into a small room with a hay bed, a chair with a tin basin on it, a shelf and some pegs. A small window looks on the lake, and the glories of the sunrises which I see from it are indescribable. Neither of my doors has a lock, and, to say the truth, neither will shut, as the wood has swelled. Below the house, on the stream which issues from the lake, there is a beautiful log dairy, with a water-wheel outside, used for churning. Besides this, there are a *corral*, a shed for the waggon, a room for the hired man, and shelters for horses and weakly calves. All these things are necessaries at this height.

The ranchmen are two Welshmen, Evans and Edwards, each with a wife and family. The men are as diverse as they can be. " Griff," as Evans is called, is short and small, and is hospitable, careless, reckless, jolly, social, convivial, peppery, good-natured, "nobody's enemy but his own." He had the wit and taste to find out Estes Park, where people have found him out, and have induced him to give them food and lodging, and add cabin to cabin to take them in. He is a splendid shot, an expert and successful hunter, a bold mountaineer, a good rider, a capital cook, and a generally "jolly fellow." His cheery laugh rings through the cabin from the early morning, and is contagious, and when the rafters ring at night with such songs as " D'ye ken John Peel ? " " Auld Lang Syne," and " John Brown," what would the chorus be without poor " Griff's" voice? What would Estes Park be without him, indeed? When he went to Denver lately we missed him as we should have missed the sunshine, and perhaps more. In the early morning, when Long's Peak is red, and the grass crackles with the hoar-frost, he arouses me with a cheery thump on my door. "We're going cattle-hunting, will you come?" or, "Will you help to drive in the cattle? you can take your pick of the horses. I want another hand." Free-hearted, lavish, popular, poor "Griff" loves liquor too well for his prosperity, and is always tormented by debt. He makes lots of money, but puts it into "a bag with holes." He has fifty horses and 1000 head of cattle, many of which are his own, wintering up here, and makes no end of money by taking in people at eight dollars a week, yet it all goes somehow. He has a most industrious wife, a girl of seventeen, and four younger children, all musical, but the wife has to work like a slave; and though he is a kind husband, her lot, as compared with her lord's, is like that of a squaw. Edwards, his partner, is his exact opposite, tall, thin, and condemnatory-looking, keen, industrious, saving, grave, a teetotaler, grieved for all reasons at Evans's follies, and rather grudging; as naturally unpopular as Evans is popular; a "decent man," who, with his industrious wife, will certainly make money as fast as Evans loses it.

I pay eight dollars a week, which includes the unlimited use of a horse, when one can be found and caught. We breakfast at seven on beef, potatoes tea, coffee, new bread, and butter. Two pitchers of cream and two of milk are replenished as fast as they are exhausted. Dinner at twelve is a repetition of the breakfast, but with the coffee omitted and a gigantic pudding added. Tea at six is a repetition of breakfast. "Eat whenever you are hungry, you can always get milk and bread in the kitchen," Evans says—"eat as much as you can, it'll do you good," and we all eat like hunters. There is no change of food. The steer which was being killed on my arrival is now being eaten through from head to tail, the meat being hacked off quite promiscuously, without any regard to joints. In this dry, rarefied air, the outside of the flesh blackens and hardens, and though the weather may be hot, the carcass keeps sweet for two or three months. The bread is super-excellent, but the poor wives seem to be making and baking it all day.

The regular household living and eating together at this time consists of a very intelligent and high-minded American couple, Mr. and Mrs. Dewy, people whose character, culture, and society I should value anywhere; a young Englishman, brother of a celebrated African traveller, who, because he rides on an English saddle, and clings to some other insular peculiarities, is called " The Earl ; " a miner prospecting for silver; a young man, the type of intelligent, practical " Young America," whose health showed consumptive tendencies when he was in business, and who is living a hunter's life here; a grown-up niece of Evans; and a melancholy-looking hired man. A mile off there is an industrious married settler, and four miles off, in the gulch leading to the Park, " Mountain Jim," otherwise Mr. Nugent, is posted. His business as a trapper takes him daily up to the beaver-dams in Black Canyon to look after his traps, and he generally spends some time in or about our cabin, not, I can see, to Evans's satisfaction. For, in truth, this blue hollow, lying solitary at the foot of Long's Peak, is a miniature world of great interest, in which love, jealousy, hatred, envy, pride, unselfishness, greed, selfishness, and self-sacrifice can be studied hourly, and there is always the unpleasantly exciting risk of an open quarrel with the neighbouring desperado, whose " I'll shoot you! " has more than once been heard in the cabin.

The party, however, has often been increased by " campers," either elk-hunters or " prospectors " for silver or locations, who feed with us and join us in the evening. They get little help from Evans, either as to elk or locations, and go away disgusted and unsuccessful. Two Englishmen of refinement and culture camped out here prospecting a few weeks ago, and then, contrary to advice, crossed the mountains into North Park, where gold is said to abound, and it is believed that they have fallen victims to the bloodthirsty Indians of that region. Of course, we never get letters or newspapers unless some one rides to Longmount for them. Two or three novels and a copy of *Our New West* are our literature. Our latest newspaper is seventeen days old. Somehow the Park seems to become the natural limit of our interests so far as they appear in conversation at table. The last grand aurora, the prospect of a snow-storm, track and sign of elk and grizzly, rumours of a bighorn herd near the lake, the canyons in which the Texan cattle were last seen, the merits of different rifles; the progress of two obvious love affairs, the probability of some one coming up from the Plains with letters, " Mountain Jim's " latest mood or escapade, and the merits of his dog " Ring " as compared with those of Evans's dog " Plunk," are among the topics which are never abandoned as exhausted.

On Sunday work is nominally laid aside, but most of the men go out hunting or fishing till the evening, when we have the harmonium and much sacred music and singing in parts. To be alone in the Park from the afternoon till the last glory of the afterglow has faded, with no books but a Bible and Prayer-book, is truly delightful. No worthier temple for a " Te Deum " or " Gloria in Excelsis " could be found than this "temple not made with hands," in which one may worship without being distracted by the sight of bonnets of endless form, and curiously intricate "back hair," and countless oddities of changing fashion.

I shall not soon forget my first night here.

Somewhat dazed by the rarefied air, entranced by the glorious beauty, slightly puzzled by the motley company, whose faces loomed not always quite distinctly through the cloud of smoke produced by eleven pipes, I went to my solitary cabin at nine, attended by Evans. It was very dark, and it seemed a long way off. Something howled—Evans said it was a wolf—and owls apparently innumerable hooted incessantly. The pole-star, exactly opposite my cabin door, burned like a lamp. The frost was sharp. Evans opened the door, lighted a candle, and left me, and I was soon in my hay bed. I was frightened—that is, afraid of being frightened, it was so eerie; but sleep soon got the better of my fears. I was awoke by a heavy breathing, a noise something like sawing under the floor, and a pushing and upheaving, all very loud. My candle was all burned, and, in truth, I dared not stir. The noise went on for an hour fully, when, just as I thought the floor had been made sufficiently thin for all purposes of ingress, the sounds abruptly ceased, and I fell asleep again. My hair was not, as it ought to have been, white in the morning!

I was dressed by seven, our breakfast-hour, and

when I reached the great cabin and told my story, Evans laughed hilariously, and Edwards contorted his face dismally. They told me that there was a skunk's lair under my cabin, and that they dare not make any attempt to dislodge him for fear of rendering the cabin untenable. They have tried to trap him since, but without success, and each night the noisy performance is repeated. I think he is sharpening his claws on the under side of my floor, as the grizzlies sharpen theirs upon the trees. The odour with which this creature, truly named Mephitis, can overpower its assailants is truly *awful*. We were driven out of the cabin for some hours merely by the passage of one across the *corral*. The bravest man is a coward in its neighbourhood. Dogs rub their noses on the ground till they bleed when they have touched the fluid, and even die of the vomiting produced by the effluvia. The odour can be smelt a mile off. If clothes are touched by the fluid they must be destroyed. At present its fur is very valuable. Several have been killed since I came. A shot well aimed at the spine secures one safely, and an experienced dog can kill one by leaping upon it suddenly without being exposed to danger. It is a beautiful beast, about the size and length of a fox, with long thick black or dark-brown fur, and two white streaks from the head to the long bushy tail. The claws of its fore-feet are long and polished. Yesterday one was seen rushing from the dairy and was shot. " Plunk," the big dog, touched it and has to be driven into exile. The body was valiantly removed by a man with a long fork, and carried to a running stream, but we are nearly choked with the odour from the spot where it fell. I hope that my skunk will enjoy a quiet spirit so long as we are near neighbours.

October 3.

This is surely one of the most entrancing spots on earth. Oh, that I could paint with pen or brush! From my bed I look on Mirror Lake, and with the very earliest dawn, when objects are not discernible, it lies there absolutely still, a purplish lead-colour. Then suddenly into its mirror flash inverted peaks, at first a bright orange, then changing into red, making the dawn darker all round. This is a new sight, each morning new. Then the peaks fade, and when morning is no longer "spread upon the mountains," the pines are mirrored in my lake almost as solid objects, and the glory steals downwards, and a red flush warms the clear atmosphere of the Park, and the hoar-frost sparkles and the crested blue jays step forth daintily on the jewelled grass. The majesty and beauty grow on me daily. As I crossed from my cabin just now, and the long mountain shadows lay on the grass, and form and colour gained new meanings, I was almost false to Hawaii; I couldn't go on writing for the glory of the sunset, but went out and sat on a rock to see the deepening blue in the dark canyons, and the peaks becoming rose colour one by one, then fading into sudden ghastliness, the awe-inspiring heights of Long's Peak fading last. Then came the glories of the afterglow, when the orange and lemon of the east faded into gray, and then gradually the gray for some distance above the horizon brightened into a cold blue, and above the blue into a broad band of rich, warm red, with an upper band of rose colour; above it hung a big cold moon. This is the "daily miracle" of evening, as the blazing peaks in the darkness of Mirror Lake are the miracle of morning. Perhaps this scenery is not lovable, but, as if it were a strong stormy character, it has an intense fascination.

The routine of my day is breakfast at seven, then I go back and "do" my cabin and draw water from the lake, read a little, loaf a little, return to the big cabin and sweep it alternately with Mrs. Dewy, after which she reads aloud till dinner at twelve. Then I ride with Mr. Dewy, or by myself, or with Mrs. Dewy, who is learning to ride cavalier fashion in order to accompany her invalid husband, or go after cattle till supper at six. After that we all sit in the living-room, and I settle down to write to you, or mend my clothes, which are dropping to pieces. Some sit round the table playing at eucre, the strange hunters and prospectors lie on the floor smoking, and rifles are cleaned, bullets cast, fishing-flies made, fishing-tackle repaired, boots are waterproofed, part-songs are sung, and about half-past eight I cross the crisp grass to my cabin, always expecting to find something in it. We all wash our own clothes, and as my stock is so small, some part of every day has to be spent at the wash-tub. Politeness and propriety always prevail in our mixed company, and though various grades of society are represented, true democratic equality prevails, not its counterfeit, and there is neither forwardness on one side nor condescension on the other.

Evans left for Denver ten days ago, taking his wife and family to the Plains for the winter, and the mirth of our party departed with him. Edwards is sombre, except when he lies on the floor in the evening, and tells stories of his march through Georgia with Sherman. I gave Evans a 100-dollar note to change, and asked him to buy me a horse for my tour, and for three days we have expected him. The mail depends on him. I have had no letters from you for five weeks, and can hardly curb my impatience. I ride or walk three or four miles out on the Longmount trail two or three times a day to look for him. Others, for different reasons, are nearly equally anxious. After dark we start at every sound, and every time the dogs bark all the able-bodied of us turn out *en masse*. "Wait for the waggon" has become a nearly maddening joke.

October 9.

The letter and newspaper fever has seized on every one. We have sent at last to Longmount. This evening I rode out on the Longmount trail towards dusk, escorted by "Mountain Jim," and in the distance we saw a waggon with four horses and a saddle-horse behind, and the driver waved a handkerchief, the concerted signal if I were the possessor of a horse. We turned back, galloping down the long hill as fast as two good horses could carry us, and gave the joyful news. It was an hour before the waggon arrived, bringing not Evans but two "campers" of suspicious aspect, who have pitched their camp close to my cabin! You cannot imagine what it is to be locked in by these mountain walls, and not to know where your letters are lying. Later on, Mr. Buchan, one of our usual inmates, returned from Denver with papers, letters for every one but me, and much exciting news. The financial panic has spread out West, gathering strength on its way. The Denver banks have all suspended business. They refuse to cash their own cheques, or to allow their customers to draw a dollar, and would not even give greenbacks for my English gold! Neither Mr. Buchan nor Evans could get a cent. Business is suspended, and everybody, however rich, is for the time being poor. The Indians have taken to the "war path," and are burning ranches and killing cattle. There is a regular "scare" among the settlers, and waggon loads of fugitives are arriving in Colorado Springs. The Indians say, "The white man has killed the buffalo and left them to rot on the plains. We will be revenged." Evans had reached Longmount, and will be here to-night.

October 10.

"Wait for the waggon" still! We had a hurricane of wind and hail last night; it was eleven before I could go to my cabin, and I only reached it with the help of two men. The moon was not up, and the sky overhead was black with clouds, when suddenly Long's Peak, which had been invisible, gleamed above the dark mountains, all glistening with new fallen snow, on which the moon, as yet unrisen here, was shining. The evening before, after sunset, I saw another novel effect. My lake turned a brilliant orange in the twilight, and in its still mirror the mountains were reflected a deep rich blue. It is a world of wonders. To-day we had a great storm with flurries of fine snow; and when the clouds rolled up at noon, the Snowy Range and all the higher mountains were pure white. I have been hard at work all day to drown my anxieties, which are heightened by a rumour that Evans has gone buffalo-hunting on the Platte!

This evening, quite unexpectedly, Evans arrived with a heavy mail in a box. I sorted it, but there was nothing for me, and Evans said he was afraid that he had left my letters, which were separate from the others, behind at Denver, but he had written from Longmount for them. A few hours later they were found in a box of groceries!

All the hilarity of the house has returned with Evans, and he has brought a kindred spirit with him, a young man who plays and sings splendidly, has an inexhaustible *repertoire*, and produces sonatas, funeral marches, anthems, reels, strathspeys, and all else, out of his wonderful memory. Never, surely, was a chamber organ compelled to such service. A little cask of suspicious appearance was smuggled into the cabin from the waggon, and heightens the hilarity a little, I fear. No churlishness could resist Evans's unutterable jollity or the contagion of his hearty laugh. He claps people on the back, shouts at them, will do anything for them, and makes a perpetual breeze. "My kingdom for a horse!" he has not got one for me, and a shadow crossed his face when I spoke of the subject. Eventually he asked for a private conference, when he told me, with some confusion, that he had found himself "very hard up" in Denver, and had been obliged to appropriate my 100-dollar note. He said he would give me, as interest for it up to November 25th, a good horse, saddle, and bridle for my proposed journey of 600 miles. I was somewhat dismayed, but there was no other course, as the money was gone.[1] I tried a horse, mended my clothes, reduced my pack to a weight of twelve pounds, and was all ready for an early start, when before daylight I was wakened by Evans's cheery voice at my door. "I say, Miss B., we've got to drive wild cattle to-day; I wish you'd lend a hand, there's not enough of us; I'll give you a good horse; one day won't make much difference." So we've been driving cattle all day, riding about twenty miles, and fording the Big Thompson about as many times. Evans flatters me by saying that I am "as much use as another man;" more than one of our party, I hope, who always avoided the "ugly" cows.

October 12.

I am still here, helping in the kitchen, driving cattle, and riding four or five times a day. Evans detains me each morning by saying, "Here's lots of horses for you to try," and after trying five or six a day, I do not find one to my liking. To-day, as I was cantering a tall well-bred one round the lake, he threw the bridle off by a toss of his head, leaving me with the reins in my hands; one bucked, and two have tender feet, and tumbled down. Such are some of our little varieties. Still I hope to get

[1] In justice to Evans, I must mention here that every cent of the money was ultimately paid, that the horse was perfection, and that the arrangement turned out a most advantageous one for me.

off on my tour in a day or two, so at least as to be able to compare Estes Park with some of the better known parts of Colorado.

You would be amused if you could see our cabin just now. There are nine men in the room and three women. For want of seats most of the men are lying on the floor; all are smoking, and the blithe young French Canadian who plays so beautifully, and catches about fifty speckled trout for each meal, is playing the harmonium with a pipe in his mouth. Three men who have camped in Black Canyon for a week are lying like dogs on the floor. They are all over six feet high, immovably solemn, neither smiling at the general hilarity, nor at the absurd changes which are being rung on the harmonium. They may be described as clothed only in boots, for their clothes are torn to rags. They stare vacantly. They have neither seen a woman nor slept under a roof for six months. Negro songs are being sung, and before that "Yankee Doodle" was played immediately after "Rule Britannia," and it made every one but the strangers laugh, it sounded so foolish and mean. The colder weather is bringing the beasts down from the heights. I heard both wolves and the mountain lion as I crossed to my cabin last night.

I. L. B.

DOCUMENTS

COLORADO AND ITS CAPITAL
by
Julian Ralph

If its people had not already called it "the Centennial State" and "the Scenic State," I might have done better by it. I would have called it the Palace-car State, because it is the only one in the West where palace-cars are run all over the tallest mountain ranges, and to the gold and silver mines as fast as they are discovered, and because the general style and finish of the cities and pleasure resorts are of palace-car luxury and thoroughness, while nature provides an endless gallery and museum of gorgeous scenery and magnificent curios that would seem extravagant anywhere else, yet are in keeping there.

Colorado is sufficiently settled and developed to form a valuable object-lesson for the study of the early results of the forces we see at work in the brand-new commonwealths near by. They are seizing the water rights in Montana, Wyoming, and Washington, but in Colorado the water is being sold and used. In the newer States wiseacres are prophesying what will be done with imperial reaches of bunch-grass and sage-brush land, but in Colorado county fairs are being held upon such lands. In Montana the leaders are wishing for an agricultural battalion of neighbors to the miners, but in Colorado agriculture has already distanced mining as a wealth-producing factor.

Denver's peculiarity and strength lie in its being all alone in the heart of a vast region between the Canadian border and the Gulf of Mexico; but it has been brought suddenly near to us. Not all the fast railway riding is done in the East these days. The far Western steeds of steel are picking up their heels in grand fashion for those who enjoy fast riding. On a palace-car train of the Union Pacific Railroad between Omaha and Denver the regular time is nearly fifty miles an hour, and the long run is made in one night, between supper and breakfast. Denver is only fifty-three hours of riding-time from New York as I write--twenty-five hours from New York to Chicago, and twenty-eight hours from Chicago to Denver.

I am going to ask the reader to spend Saturday and Sunday in Denver with me. Instead of dryly cataloguing what is there, we will see it for ourselves. I had supposed it to be a mountain city, so much does an Eastern man hear of its elevation, its mountain resorts, and its mountain air. It surprised me to discover that it was a city of the plains. There is nothing in the appearance of the plains to lead one to suppose that they tilt up like a toboggan slide, as they do, or that Denver is a mile above sea-level, as it is. But a part of its enormous good fortune is that although it is a plains city, it has the mountains for near neighbors-- a long peaked and scalloped line of purple or pink or blue or snow-clad green, according to when they are viewed. There are 200 miles or more of the Rockies in sight in clear weather. As there are but fifty-six cloudy days in the year, and as these mountains elevate and inspire even the dullest souls, I think we can forget that it is a city of the plains, and ever associate it with the mountains hereafter. I plighted my troth to the sea near which I was born, but in Denver and Salt Lake City, loveliest of all our inland cities, I felt a straining at my loyalty; and when I saw in the diningroom of Mr. W.N. Byers the great square window that his charming wife ordered made so that she might frame 200 miles of the Rockies as in a picture, I admitted to myself that there was much to be said for "t'other dear charmer," and that, in the language of Denver's poet, Cy Warman, "God was good to make the mountains."

We have looked on Denver's patent map, and know where we are. Every Western city has its own patent map, usually designed to show that it is in the centre of creation, but Denver's map is more truthful, and merely locates it in the middle of the country west of the Mississippi. It shows the States east of that river without a single railroad, while a perfect labyrinth of railroads crisscross the West in frantic efforts to get to Denver. Gravely a Denver man says to us afterward, as he holds the map in his hand, "If those Dutchmen and Puritans and things who settled the East could have landed out here on the plains, the thirteen original colonies would have been a howling wilderness filled with savages to-day." And that in turn reminds me of the remark of a man in Utah, a Mormon, who was a member of a colony that pre-empted an alkali lake, washed out the salt with a system of ditches, and succeeded in growing crops. "Eastern people make a great mouth about irrigation and farming in the arid belt," said he, "but we folks 'd rather scoop out a ditch than have to clear out forest stumps and blast rocks to get room for farming." The moral of both these tales is that we may have our own opinion of the West, but we can't prevent the West's having its own opinion of us.

In all other respects the patent Denver map is reliable. It shows that this city of 135,000 souls stands all alone, without a real rival in a vast rich region. It is 1000 miles from Chicago, 400 from Salt Lake City, 600 from Kansas City, and the same distance from the Missouri River. If you drew a circle of 1000 miles diameter, with Denver in its centre, you would discover no real competitor; but the people have adopted what they call their "thousand-mile theory," which is that Chicago is 1000 miles from New York, and Denver is 1000 miles from Chicago, and San Francisco is 1000 miles from Denver, so that, as any one can see, if great cities are put at that distance apart, as it seems, then these are to be the four great ones of America.

Denver is a beautiful city--a parlor city with cabinet finish--and it is so new that it looks as if it had been made to order, and was just ready for delivery. How the people lived five years ago, or what they have done with the houses of that period, does not appear, but at present everything--business blocks, churches, clubs, dwellings, street cars, the park--all look brand-new, like the young trees. The first citizen you talk to says, "You notice there are no old people on the streets here. There aren't any in the city. We have no use for old folks here." So, then, the people also are new. It is very wonderful and peculiar.

Only a year ago Mr. Richard Harding Davis was there and commented on the lack of pavements in the streets, and I hear that at that time pedestrians wore rubber boots, and the mud was frightful. But now every street in the thick of town is paved with concrete or Belgian blocks as well as if it were New York or Paris. The first things that impress you in the city are the neatness and width of the streets, and the number of young trees that ornament them most invitingly. The next thing is the remarkable character of the big business buildings. It is not that they are bigger and better than those of New York and Chicago--comparisons of that sort are nonsensical--but they are massive and beautiful, and they possess an elegance without and a roominess and lightness within that distinguish them as superior to the show buildings of most of the cities of the country. The hotels are even more remarkable, from the one down by the impressive big depot, which is the best-equipped third-class hotel in the country, to the Brown's Palace and the Metropole, both of steel and stone, which are just as good as men know how to make hotels.

    The residence districts are of a piece with the rest. Along the tree-lined streets are some of the very prettiest villas it is any man's lot to see at this time. They are not palaces, but they are very tasteful, stylish, cozy, and pretty homes, all built of brick or stone, in a great variety of pleasing colors and materials, and with a proud showing of towers, turrets, conservatories, bay-windows, gables, and all else that goes to mark this period, when men build after widely differing plans to compliment their own taste and the skill of originating draughtsmen. The town spreads over an enormous territory, as compared with the space a city of its size should take up, but we must learn that modern methods of quick transit are so cheap that they are being adopted everywhere, and wherever they are used the cities are spreading out. Denver has cable and electric cars, but it is the electric roads that are the city-spreaders. They whiz along so fast that men do not hesitate to

build their homes five or six miles from their stores
and offices where they can get garden and elbow room.
We are going to see all our cities shoot out in this
way. It promotes beauty in residence districts, and
pride in the hearts of those who own the pretty homes.
It carries the good health that comes with fresh air.
But it entails a great new expense upon modern city
government, for the streets and the mains and sewers
and police and fire systems all have to be extended to
keep pace with the electric flight of the people, who,
in turn, must stand the taxes. Not that they are high
in Denver, or in those other electric-car-peppered
capitals, Minneapolis and St. Paul, but they are
higher than they would be if the people were crowded
into smaller spaces. In Denver the government has
spared itself and the people one source of anxiety by
ordering that, no matter where the houses reach to, it
shall be a fire-proof city. The fire lines follow the
extension, and every house must be of brick or stone.

As we walk about the town, noting the theatres
that are absolutely gorgeous, observing that the
Methodist church is a quarter-of-a-million-dollar pile
of granite, seeing the crowded shopping stores that
are almost like our own in New York, heeding the bustle
of people and vehicles, stopping to look at the precious
Colorado stones that are heaped in the jewellers'
windows, and the museums of Indian curios that are
peculiar to the town, a marked and distinctive secret
of the place is forced upon our attention. It is that
though the signs of great wealth and liberal outlay are
in every view, there is no over-decoration, no vulgar
display, no wasteful ostentation (except in that
saloon that has silver dollars sunk in the floor, and
that other one where the mosaic floor slabs are set
with double eagles). There is upon the showplaces of
the town that restraint which we call "taste." To be
sure the barrooms cost the price of a prince's
ransom, and the walls and bars are made of onyx.
But there they stop. A little spray of silver arabesquerie, necessary to save such a room from bareness,
is all the ornament one sees. In the high-class hotels,

for some reason that appears inscrutable to an American who has been surfeited with bold paintings and dubious bric-a-brac from Madison Square to Nob Hill, there is the same extraordinary good taste. The walls of all the rooms, both public and private, rely on the harmonious blending of soft tints, and on mere lines of fine beading on the hardwood fittings. Why that taste which makes the apartments of the Japanese our marvel and delight should reappear in Denver, and nowhere else out West, is certainly remarkable.

"There is in Denver," says a man who meets me in the Hotel Metropole, "what is shockingly called 'the one-lunged army.' I am a member of it, and may repeat the nickname without shame, for we are proud of ourselves. This army comprises 30,000 invalids, or more than one-fifth of the population of Denver. Not by any means is this a host of persons with pulmonary ailments, but of men in physical straits of many sorts, who find the rare air of a place a mile on the road to heaven better than medicine. These are men of wealth, as a rule, and of cultivation and of taste. They have been more important factors in the making of this unique city than most persons, even in Denver, imagine. The stock and oil and gold and silver millionaires point to their operations as the cause of Denver's importance; and they are right. But importance is one thing, and good taste, good society, and progressiveness are quite different things. It was not mining that begot the taste which crowds our residence quarter with elegant dwellings, or that created a demand for clubs like the Denver Club. It was not oil that gave us college-bred men to form a Varsity Club of 120 members, or that insisted upon the decoration of the town with such hotels as ours. The influence of the invalids is seen in all this. They are New-Yorkers, Bostonians, Philadelphians, New Orleans men, Englishmen--the well-to-do and well-brought-up men from all over the country--architects, doctors, lawyers, and every sort of professional men being among them."

After that we caught ourselves constantly looking for invalids, but without success. Even those who told us that they were members of the strange army of debilitated aesthetes did not look so. But we came upon many queer facts regarding them, and the air, and the customs of the place. One very noticeable peculiarity of the people was their habit of speaking of the East as "home." "At home in the East we call that Virginia-creeper," said one. "I can go home to New York every few months," said another. "We long to go back East to our homes, but when we get there the climate does not agree with us, and we hurry back to Colorado." Thus was revealed the peculiar tenure the place has upon thousands of its citizens. But among them are very many who say that it is customary for Eastern folks to let their regard for the East keep warm until the moment comes when they seriously consider the idea of leaving Colorado. At that juncture they realize for the first time the magic of the mountain air and the hold it has upon them. Few indeed ever seriously think of leaving it after one such consultation with themselves. But I must say it is a very queer air. It keeps every one keyed up to the trembling-point, inciting the population to tireless, incessant effort, like a ceaseless breathing-in of alcohol. It creates a highly nervous people, and, as one man said, "it is strange to fancy what the literature of Colorado will be when it develops its own romancers and poets, so strong is the nervous strain and mental exaltation of the people." One would suppose alcohol unnecessary here; but, on the contrary, there is much drinking. It is a dangerous indulgence. Among the dissolutes suicides are frequent. "If you stay here a week you will read of two," said a citizen. And I did. It was found that when the saloons were allowed to remain open all night, violent crimes were of frequent occurrence. Drinking too deep and too long was the cause. The saloons were therefore ordered shut at twelve o'clock, and a remarkable decrease of these crimes followed.

We shall see that on its worst side the city is Western, and that its moral side is Eastern. It will be interesting to see how one side dominates the other, and both keep along together. But in the mean time what is most peculiar is the indifference with which the populace regards murder among these gamblers and desperadoes who are a feature of every new country, and who are found in Denver, though, I suspect, the ladies and children never see them, so well separated are the decent and the vicious quarters. It is said that not very long ago it was the tacit agreement of the people that it was not worth while to put the county to the cost or bother of seriously pursuing, prosecuting, and hanging or imprisoning a thug who murdered another thug. It was argued that there was one bad man less, and that if the murderer was at large another one would kill him. The axiom that "only bad men are the victims of bad men" obtained there, as it did in Cheyenne and Deadwood, and does in Butte. To-day a murder in a dive or gambling-hell excited little comment and no sensation in Denver, and I could distinctly see a trace of the old spirit in the speech of the reputable men when I talked to them of the one crime of the sort that took place while I was there.

The night side of the town is principally corralled, as they say; that is, its disorderly houses are all on one street. There is another mining-town characteristic--wide-open gambling. The "hells" are mainly abovestairs, over saloons. The vice is not flaunted as it is in certain other cities; but once in the gambling-places, the visitor sees them to be like those my readers became acquainted with in Butte, Montana--great open places, like the board-rooms in our stock exchanges, lined with gambling lay-outs. They are crowded on this Saturday night with rough men in careless dress or in the apparel of laborers. These are railroad employees, workers from the nearest mines, laborers, clerks--every sort of men who earn their money hard, and think to make more out of it by letting it go easily. Roulette, red and black, and faro are games. Behind each table sits the imperturbable dealer--sometimes a rough cowboyish-looking young man, who had

left off his necktie so as to show his diamond stud;
sometimes a man who would pass for a gray-bearded deacon in a village church. By each dealer's side sits
the "lookout," chewing a cigar, and lazily looking on
in the interests of such fair play as is consistent
with professional gambling. All around each table, except on the dealer's side, crowd the idiots, straining
and pushing to put their chips where luck will perch.
These places are orderly, of course. It is the rule
with them everywhere. There is very little conversation.
Except for the musical clink-link-link of the ivory
chips, the shuffling of feet, and the rattle of the
roulette marbles, there is little noise. But the floor
boards hold small sea-beds of expectoration, and over
each table is enough tobacco smoke to beget the fancy
that each lay-out is a mouth of the pit of hell.

Queer characters illustrate queer stories in
these places, just as they do in the mining regions,
but with the difference that all the stories of luck
in the mines are cast with characters who are either
rich or "broke," while in the hells they seem never to
be in luck when you happen on them. They were flush
yesterday, and will be to-morrow--if you will "stake"
them with something to gamble with. The man who once
had a bank of his own and the one who broke the biggest
bank in Leadville were mere ordinary *dramatis personae*
when I looked in, but the towering giant of the place
was the man who at twenty-six years of age had killed
twenty-six men, all so justly, however, that he never
stood trial for one episode. This is part of the "local color" in any picture of Denver; but, on the other
hand, the best of that color is, as I have hinted, of
the tone of lovely firesides, elegance, wealth and
refinement.

From the gaming to the fruit fair that happens
to be in progress, we are eager to go. The fruit or
orchard exhibition was an unlooked-for consummation in
so new a State. It was a sight of the dawn of the
fruit industry where the best orchards were not five
years old. Indeed, some of the finest fruit was

plucked where Indians were guarded not long before. There were apples, pears, peaches, plums, quinces, grapes, and ground-cherries. It was too late in the year (October) for berries, but they are grown in Colorado in great abundance, and the strawberries are said to be big and most delicious. The fruits I saw displayed at the fair were of large though not California size. Their most remarkable quality to the eye was their gorgeous coloring--the richest and deepest I ever saw except in paintings. I found afterwards that all the fruit grown in the valleys of the Rockies is equally gorgeous. But of more practical import is the fact that this Colorado fruit is of delicious flavor. In Denver and in other parts of the State I tasted every product of the orchards. I cannot recall my experience in California clearly enough to say more than that they pick their fruit green to ship it away, and so they miss the credit they deserve abroad as growers of luscious fruit. I would like to encourage the Coloradans in their boast that theirs has higher flavor than the west-coast product (if it were true, and I had both kinds to prove it by), and I will say that I think I never enjoyed any fruit any more than most of that which I ate in Colorado. The only melons at the show were muskmelons, but it is a great State for melons, particularly for watermelons. One place, Rocky Ford, in Otero County, is celebrated for its observance of what is called "melon day" every year, when the idle people, tourists, and pleasure--seekers gather there to eat free melons in a great amphitheatre built for that purpose. This affair is not altogether unique. At Monument, in Douglas County, the exuberant villagers dig a great trench and cook potatoes--as the Rhode-Islanders do clams--for the multitude, without charge. The fruit at the Denver show was grown in the following counties: Arapahoe, Boulder, Delta, Grand, Jefferson, Larimer, Mesa, Montrose, Otereo, and Weld.

The wild flowers at this show were very interesting. No account of Colorado would be complete if it omitted at least some mention of these gorgeous ornaments which Nature litters with lavish hands all over the State--far up the mountain-sides, where the very rocks are stained with rich colors, and up and down the valleys, where even man's importation, the alfalfa, turns the ranches into great blue beds of thickly clustered blossoms. It may have been the flowers, or it may have been the beautifully stained rocks, or, as some say, the color of the water in the Colorado River, that gained the State the Spanish name it bears, but whichever it was, the flowers alone were sufficient to justify the christening, so multitudinous, lovely, varied, and gay are they. Fortunately for the fame of the flowers, certain Colorado ladies are skilled in pressing them so as to reproduce and preserve the natural poses of all the flowering plants, as well as to make them retain their colors unimpaired. The work of these women is now known in every part of the civilized world.

It was interesting to read the progress of Denver in the remarks of those who were presented to me during that visit to the fruit show. One gentleman was interested in the electric-light plant, and said that it is so powerful that during a recent decoration of the streets in honor of a convention that was held there, no less than 22,000 incandescent and four 5000 candle-power search-lights were used in the display. In few cities in the world, he said, is this light so generally and so lavishly used. He added that few of the dwellings, except in the poorest quarter, are without telephones.

A public official volunteered the information that since 1870 the percentage of increase of population has been greater in Denver than in any other city of the land, it being something more than 2000 per cent. A bevy of smiling young women was pointed out as representative art students; for there is a Denver Art League which has sixty members, and aims to maintain classes in oil and watercolor work and sculpture. Two of the classes, one for each sex, pursue the practice of drawing and painting from the nude. This institution is the pride and care of the leading business and professional men of the city, who give it ample funds, and are encouraged by the eagerness of the youth of the State, as well as of the city, to enjoy its advantages. A merchant spoke of the Chamber of Commerce, to the enterprise and kindness of which, and especially of the secretary, I was afterward indebted. I learned that this watchful organization of promoters of the commercial welfare of the city maintains a fine free library, containing a collection of books that now numbers 20,000 volumes, and is constantly increasing. No less than 77,000 volumes were read in the homes of its patrons last year. The reading-room is kept open on all the days of the year, and the city government has passed an ordinance appropriating $500 a month, from the fines imposed by the police magistrates, for the benefit of this valuable institution. Another new acquaintance urged me to see the public schools of the city. The high-school building cost $325,000, and is the second most costly and complete one in existence. Many of the ward or district schools cost a fifth, and some cost more than a fifth, of that large sum. I could not then nor there farther insist upon the opinions that have engendered the only criticisms that have passed between myself in these papers and the new West which I am describing. The report of the Denver Board of Education is before me, and if I read it aright, it declares that the common-school system embraces a course of twelve years of study, eight in the common schools and four in the high-school. Drawing, music, physical culture, and German are mentioned as among the studies in the grammar grades, while the wide gamut between algebra and Greek, with military training for the boys, comprises the high-school course. The 700 high-school pupils are said to be of the average age of seventeen years. I reiterate that this is education for the well-to-do at the expense of the poor. If Denver is like any other town of my acquaintance, the poor cannot release their children from toil during twelve years after they are of an age to be sent to school. The disparity between the sum of 9500 in the common schools and the sum of 700 in the high-school makes it appear that Denver is no exception to the rule. I will not dwell upon my belief that the wide range of studies in these latter-day schools gives children a mere but dangerous smattering of many things and no thorough grounding in any study, and that the result is to produce a distaste for honest labor and an unfitness for anything above it. It is unpleasant to criticise at all where a community is so enthusiastic as this, but I believe the whole system, whether we find it in New York and Boston, as we do, or in Denver, is undemocratic, unjust, and unwise. The "little red school-house on the hill," which has been glorified as the chief pride of Puritan New England, is the seed that has grown into the $300,000 palace of learning for 700 children, at the expense of the parents of more than 9000 other children. The little red school-house was grand indeed. It taught the "three R's" thoroughly, and when a boy or girl wanted more, he or she managed to get it, at such pains and in such a way as to cause him or her to value all that was acquired. Honest work was the portion of all but the rich, who paid for their children's higher schooling. However, the spirit in which Denver maintains and elaborates her school system is beyond all criticism; it is, indeed, creditable and wonderful. If we do not agree about the result, I can at least testify to the impression I received--that the whole people are honestly and enthusiastically proud of their schools, and that of their elaborate kind they are among the best in the country.

Denver has other than her public schools--the (Methodist) University of Denver, the (Catholic) St. Mary's Academy, the (Episcopal) St. John's College for boys; an Episcopal school for girls, called Wolfe Hall; the Woman's College, and the Westminster University, the first a Baptist and the second a Presbyterian institution. I should have mentioned the fact that a second fine public library is maintained in connection with the public-school system. It goes without saying, in a study of a city like Denver, that musical, dramatic, literary, and kindred coteries are numerous.

Away from the fruit display, out in the brightly lit streets, were the crowds of Saturday-night shoppers. Of these many more were persons employed in manufacturing industries than those would imagine who know no more of Denver than I have told. The fine and varied building stones that will yet become a great asset in Colorado's inventory of wealth are cut and dressed in more than one establishment. The notable buildings of Denver are built of Colorado red sandstone, granite, and other beautiful materials found in the mountains. The main or parent range of the Rockies loses its striking configuration soon after leaving Colorado in the south. Then it becomes a broken, ragged chain. They have some good stones in the territories to the southward, but not the assortment found in Colorado. Already Colorado stones are shipped to Chicago, the Nebraska and Kansas towns, and Texas. These are brownstones, granite, a so-called lava or metamorphic stone of great durability and beauty, and a variety of sandstones. Some red sandstone that I saw being quarried in the Dolores Valley, where it is abundant beyond calculation, is said to be well adapted for fine interior decorative uses. Others in the crowds were workers in the cotton factory; in a knitting-mill that has been removed there from the East; in the three large establishments where preserves, fruit pickles, and sauces are made; in the making of fire-brick, drain-pipe, jugs, churns, and other coarse pottery; in the manufacture of the best mining machinery in the world, whole outfits of which have been shipped to China and South Africa, to say nothing of Mexico and our own mining regions, which are all supplied from Denver. Other operatives work upon the hoisting machinery and pumping machines, of which the Denver patterns are celebrated. Still others in the streets work at the stock-yards, where there are two large packing companies, and where nearly 200,000 hogs, cattle, and sheep were slaughtered last year. A mill for the manufacture of news paper has been in operation for a year, and now (October, '92) three other paper-mills are about to be erected, the aim being to make book and letter paper, Manilas, coarse wrapping-paper, and flooring and roofing papers, as well as to produce the pulp used in these manufactures.

The three smelting-works employ nearly 400 men, and handled 400,000 tons of ore, producing $24,500,000 in gold, silver, lead, and copper last year. In addition to the twenty foundries and machine shops of whose work I have spoken, there are thirty other iron-working establishments, making tin and sheet-iron work and wire-work. In another year a barbed-wire factory and a wire and nail making plant will be in operation. There are sixty brick-making firms. Leather-workers are numerous, but all the leather is imported; there is no tannery here. Paint and white-lead making are large industries; there are six breweries; and eight firms engage in wood-working and the making of building material. In a sentence, this busy metropolis is manufacturing for the vast territory around it, with 339 manufacturing establishments, employing 9000 operatives, and producing $46,000,000 worth of goods.

The Chamber of Commerce advertises the need of woolen mills, stocking factories, tanneries, boot and shoe factories, glue factories, and potteries, but declares that Denver will give no subsidies to get them. "The natural advantages of the centre of a region as large as the German Empire, without a rival for 600 miles in any direction, combined with cheap fuel, fine climate, abundant supply of intelligent labor at reasonable prices, unutilized local raw materials, a good and evergrowing local market, protected against Eastern competition by from 1000 to 2000 miles of railroad haul--these are the inducements that Denver offers to new manufacturing plants."

And now we will fancy it is Sunday in Denver. The worshippers are coming out of the churches. But in the streets rush the cable cars with their week-day clanging of bells. On the car roofs are the signs, "To Elitch's Gardens," where, according to the papers next day, there are "the music and dancing and bangle-bedizened women." Other cars rush toward the City

Park, where the State Capital Band is to play. "Oho!" thought the critical Eastern visitors; "we are in the presence of the usual American Sunday, with the gin-mills and the gambling-places all wide open." No so. So far as I could see, not a bar-room was open. The shades were up, and the desolate interiors were in plain view from the streets. The gambling-saloons were tight shut. No one loitered near them. Here, then, had reappeared the Sunday of the Atlantic coast, for the local ordinances are enforced, and require the closing of the saloons and "hells" from Saturday midnight until Monday morning.

Except for the cling-clang of the street cars, an Eastern-Sunday hush was upon the town. Just as we see them in New York, country couples, strangers there, walked arm in arm in the business quarter, looking in the shop windows; German families, children and all, in stiff Sunday best, streamed along in queues behind the fathers; idle young men with large cigars leaned against the corners and the corner lamp-posts, and the business streets were nine-tenths dead. Thousands gathered in the park, just as they do on such a Sunday in New York. Beyond that the silence and stagnation of Sunday were on the town. In the Denver Club the prosperous men loafed about, and looked in at the great round table in the private dining-room with thoughts of the grand dinners it had borne. In the pretty homes were many circles wherein the West was discussed just as it is in New York, with sharp words for its gambling, its pistol-carrying, and its generally noisy Sundays. It was strange to hear in the West such talk of the West. It was easy to see the source of the influence that brought about that quiet day of worship. Yet in the same homes, in the same circles, was heard the most fulsome lauding of Denver and Colorado--praise that seemed to lift those altitudinous places even nearer to the clouds. With only the happiest memories and kindest wishes, then, adieu to Denver.

THE JUVENILE COURT
by
Ben B. Lindsey

It was with a saddened pride, at last, that I took my place on the bench. I had dropped my partnership with Senator Gardner. I had only nine months of office before me. And already my party had turned against me and my prospects of any future as a judge were as blank as despair.

However, the mills of Justice began to grind; and I was there to see that everything in the hopper passed truly between the stones. Sitting behind a desk that looked as if it had been designed as a wooden sepulchre, I acted as public umpire in will cases that involved interminable petty family quarrels, or in real-estate cases where one long file of witnesses swore to the falseness of the testimony of another file equally long, or in divorce proceedings for non-support, tiresomely formal and undefended usually (probably because they had been prearranged), or in involved and technical disputes between landlords and tenants, debtors and creditors, purchasers and agents. Many of the trials were jury trials, and I was no more than a judicial automation on a dais, obliged to give my decision according to the findings of the jury. Many of the cases involved property of so little value that it would not pay the fees of the empassioned lawyers employed to dispute its ownership; and these cases dragged along for days, till I felt like a man tied to a chair and compelled to listen forever to "a tale told by an idiot, full of sound and fury, signifying nothing."

(I had often admired in some wise old judge the Olympian air of detachment with which he listened to the recital of the human tragedies that were arraigned before him, as if he were above mortality and as indifferent as fate. I understood, now, as the judge of a county court, and have been slowly bored to dessication.)

One winter afternoon, after I had been listening for days to one of these cases--if I remember rightly, it concerned the ownership of some musty old mortgaged furniture that had been stored in a warehouse and was claimed by the mortgagee on the mortgage and by the warehouseman on a storage lien--the Assistant District Attorney interrupted the proceedings to ask me if I would not dispose of a larceny case that would not take two minutes. I was willing. He brought in a boy, whom I shall call "Tony Costello,"* and arraigned him before the court. The Clerk read the indictment; a railroad detective gave his testimony; the boy was accused of stealing coal from the tracks, and he had no defense. Frightened and silent, he stood looking from me to the jury, from the jury to the attorney, and from the attorney back to me--big-eyed and trembling--a helpless infant, trying to follow in our faces what was going on. The case was clear. There was nothing for me to do under the law but to find him guilty and sentence him to a term in the State Reform School. I did it--and prepared to go back to the affair of the second-hand furniture.

There had been sitting in the back of the courtroom an old woman with a shawl on her head, huddled up like a squaw, wooden-faced, and incredibly wrinkled. She waddled down the aisle toward the bench, while papers of commitment were being made out against the boy, and began to talk to the court interpreter in an excited gabble which I did not understand. I signed to the counsel for the warehouseman to proceed with his case; he rose--and he was greeted with the most soul-piercing scream of agony that I ever heard from a human throat. The old woman stood there, clutching her shawl to her breast, her toothless mouth open, her face as contorted as if she were being torn limb from limb, shrieking horribly. She threw her hands up to her head, grasped her poor, thin gray hair, and pulled it, yelling, with protruding eyes, like a madwomen. When the bailiff of the court caught hold of her to take

---

*This name, and those of all other children brought before the court, are disguised in order to protect the families from the consequences of publicity.

her from the room, she broke away from him and ran to the wall and beat her head against it, as if she would batter the court house down on us all and bury our injustice under the ruins. They dragged her out into the hall, but through the closed door I could still hear her shrieking--shrieking terribly. I adjourned the court and retreated to my chambers, very much shaken and unnerved; but I still heard her, in the hall, wailing and sobbing, and every now and then screaming as if her heart was being torn out of her.

    I did not know what to do. I thought I had no power, under the law, to do anything but what I *had* done. The boy was guilty. The law required that I should sentence him. The mother might scream herself dumb, but I was unable to help her.

    She continued to scream. Two reporters, attracted by the uproar, came to ask me if I could not do something for her. I telephoned the District Attorney and asked him whether I could not change my order against the boy--make it a suspended sentence--and let me look into the case myself. He was doubtful--as I was--about my right to do such a thing, but I accepted the responsibility of the act and he consented to it. After what seemed an hour to me--during which I could still hear the miserable woman wailing--the boy returned to her and she was quieted.

    Then I took the first step toward founding the Juvenile Court of Denver. I got an officer who knew Tony, and I went with him, at night, to the boy's home in the Italian quarter of North Denver. I need not describe the miserable conditions in which I found the Costellos living--in two rooms, in a filthy shack, with the father sick in bed, and the whole family struggling against starvation. I talked with Tony, and found him not a criminal, not a bad boy, but merely a boy. He had seen that his father and his mother and the baby were suffering from cold, and he had brought home fuel from the railroad tracks to keep them warm. I gave him a little lecture on the necessity of obeying the laws, and put him "on probation." The mother kissed my hands. The neighbors came in to salute me and to rejoice with the Costellos. I left them. But I carried away with me what must have been something of their view of my court and my absurd handling of their boy; and I began to think over this business of punishing infants as if they were adults and of maiming young lives by trying to make the gristle of their unformed characters carry the weight of our iron laws and heavy penalties.

(Let me add, in parentheses, that I saw, too, in the Costello home, the trail of the Beast. The father was ill of lead-poisoning from working twelve hours a day in a smelter. If society had done its duty by protecting him from the rapacity of his employer--by means of an eight-hour law and an employer's liability law--his son would not have been driven to steal.)

Some days later, when I opened court in the morning, the Clerk told me we had a burglary case to try. I looked about for the burglars. Three small boys, all still in their teens, were arraigned before me, their little freckled faces swollen with tears. They had broken into a barn on Arapahoe Street and had stolen pigeons from a man named Fay. The name startled me. "Fay?" I asked. He was pointed out to me in the court room. I knew him. It was the same man.

It was the same man whose pigeons I had once started out to steal, with three other youngsters, years before, when I was no bigger than the smallest tow-head who stood whimpering before me. I had not had "sand enough" to follow into the barn--it was the same barn--but at the time I had not thought *that* weakness to my credit, and neither had my companions. But "burglary"? It had been mere mischief, an adventure, a boy's way of plaguing old Fay whom we considered the "grouchy" enemy of all boys.

"I don't think these children should be charged with burglary," I said to the Clerk, rather shamefacedly. "Bring them into my chambers."

They came, and I confronted in their small persons the innocent crimes of my own "kid" days. They told me all about their "burglary," their feud with Fay--whom two of the boys accused of having taken *their* pigeons--and their boyish indignation against him for having called in the cops in the quarrel. I lectured them--as self-righteously as I could remember the circumstances--and discharged them on suspended sentence, with a warning.

I went to the Clerk of the Court, Mr. Hubert L. Shattuck. "This is all wrong," I said. "It's all nonsense--bringing these children in here on criminal charges--to be punished--sentenced to prison--degraded for life!"

"Well, Judge," he explained, "we sometimes get short on our fee accounts, and it helps to increase fees in this office to bring the kids here."

It did. The officers of the court were paid so much for each conviction obtained by the court. They received no regular salaries. When they wished to make up arrears of pay, they rounded up a batch of youngsters and "put them through." The same thing was done in the police court, the court of the justice of the peace, and the criminal court.

It was more than absurd, more than wrong. It was an outrage against childhood, against society, against justice, decency and common sense. I began to search statutes for the laws in the matter, to frequent the jails in order to see how the children were treated there, to compile statistics of the cost to the county of these trials and the cost to society of this way of making criminals of little children. And the deeper I went into the matter, the more astounded I became.

I found boys in the city jail, in cells reeking with filth and crawling with vermin, waiting trial for some such infantile offences as these I have described. I found boys in the county jail locked up with men of the vilest immorality, listening to obscene stories, subject to the most degrading personal indignities, and taking lessons in a high school of vice with all the receptive eagerness of innocence. I found that the older boys, now almost confirmed in viciousness, had begun their careers as Tony Costello had, or these burglars of the pigeon roost. And I found that many of the hardened criminals were merely the perfect graduates of the system of which I had been a sort of proud superintendent.

It kept me awake all night. It possessed me with a remorseful horror. I went about talking, "agitating," investigating, pestering the jailers, spending my Sundays in the cells among the criminals, trying to draft reform laws and in every way making myself a nuisance to everybody. I put into this work all the balked enthusiasm that my unsuccessful legislative reforms had left me. I could help the children, if I could not help the "grown-ups."

Some of these "grown-ups," whom my activities annoyed, began to say I was "crazy." Our family physician came, on that report, to remonstrate with me. A relative, very much alarmed, asked me to be careful of myself, not to "overdo." And I felt as if I were standing before a burning building, with children crying for help in the flames at the upper windows, while my friends remonstrated: "Be calm. Don't excite yourself so. People will think you're not sane!"

Not sane? Well it depends on what you consider "sane." One very sane thing to do would have been to turn my back on the fire and the children perishing in it, blame the inefficiency of the fire department, shrug a shoulder as if to say: "Well, it's none of my business," and go home to my dinner. I know *that* sort of sanity. I have seen it, many times, myself. But in the transports of my so-called insanity, I found a section of the Colorado school law of April 12, 1899, by means of which I could get a ladder up to those doomed children. And this was it:

"Section 4. Every child . . . who does not attend school . . . or who is in attendance at any school and is vicious, incorrigible, or immoral in conduct, or who is an habitual truant from school, or who habitually wanders about the streets during school hours without any lawful occupation or employment, or who habitually wanders about the streets in the night time . . . shall be deemed a *juvenile disorderly person* and be subject to the provisions of this act."

A juvenile disorderly person! Not a criminal to be punished under the criminal law, but a ward of the state, to be corrected by the state as *parens patriae*. The law was a school law, intended only for the disciplining of school children; but it could be construed as I proceeded to construe it. It was not a steel fire-escape built according to the statutory regulations. It was merely a wooden ladder rotting in a back yard. But it would reach the lower stories-- and I asked the District Attorney in future to file all his complaints against children under this law, in my court, according to a form which I furnished--and he agreed to do so. Thus our "juvenile court" was begun informally, anonymously, so to speak, but effectually. It was, as far as I knew, the first juvenile court in America and the simple beginning of a reform that has since gone round the world.*

We had still to evolve some system of handling the children. We needed, above all, probation officers; and--proceeding still under the school law--I went to all the school boards, asking for the appointment of truant officers whom I could use in the court. I addressed meetings of schoolteachers, harangued women's clubs, Christian associations, charitable societies and church meetings, boring people with "the problem of the children" wherever I could get leave to speak. All this slowly aroused a public enthusiasm that was to become in time very powerful; it attracted attention to the court and helped me with the parents of delinquent children. It brought in subscriptions from public-spirited men and women to help on the "good work." It prepared for the passage of the necessary laws which I was drafting for the next session of the Legislature. And it led me, finally, as you shall see, into another collision with the Beast.

Meanwhile, however, a more imminent collision was impending.

---

*Chicago is technically entitled to the honour of having founded the first juvenile court so-called-- under a law effective in June, 1899, two months after the approval of the law under which I worked.

A reform movement had been started in Denver against the liquor "dives," or "wine-rooms," as they were called. There was a law on the statute books forbidding saloons to serve liquor to women, but a great part of the trade of the dives was done with prostitutes, and all the places were fitted up with "cribs" and "private tooms" where young girls could be drugged and ruined and the "white-slave" traffic promoted. The wine-room keepers were backed, of course, by the political power of the brewers, and the inmates were used by the System on election day as repeaters, ballot-box stuffers, and poll thugs, as they are in so many of our cities. So, when the reform movement against the "wine-room evil" became so dangerously strong that the members of the Fire and Police Board saw that they would either have to enforce the law or involve the Democratic party in the danger of defeat, a dive keeper named Cronin was put forward in an appeal to the court for protection from the police. He was defended by Milton Smith, who was chairman of our Democratic State Central Committee. From a prosecution in a police magistrate's court, Cronin was brought before District Judge Peter L. Palmer, whose record needs no remark. And Judge Palmer promptly granted **an injunction restraining the magistrate and the Fire** and Police Board from prosecuting Cronin--grounding his decision on the delicious argument that the "wine-room law" was an infringement of the constitutional rights of women. The ministers who censured him were summoned before him and silenced with threats for contempt of court. Cronin went back to his dive; the Fire and Police Board was rescued from an awkward position; and the wine-rooms threw their doors wide open again to seduction.

I was interested in the affair because I had seen how many of the young girls brought before me had been ruined in wine-rooms. I had jurisdiction in the case because my court was the court of appeal from the magistrate's court in which the test proceedings against Cronin had been begun. And I went out of my way to bring some friendly pressure to bear on the Deputy City Attorney to get him to file an appeal in my court.

He did it; and before the case was called I was visited in my chambers by another member of our Democratic County Executive Committee, who was also an agent for the brewers' trust. He wished to speak to me about the Cronin matter. "You know, Judge," he said, "there's a liberal element in this town that controls about 10,000 votes. If we offend them in this wine-room business, they'll hook up with the Republicans this fall, and we'll lose the elections. I know you're a good Democrat the same as I am, and I know you don't want to put the party in a hole. I'm interested in you. I want to see you succeed. I want to see you renominated and reelected, and I know you can't do it with this liberal element against you. Can you? Well, now, Judge Palmer has fixed this Cronin case all right. You can leave it with him, as it stands, and no one can say a word against you. It's up to him. If there's any kick from the church people, it's coming to *him*. Let *him* take it." And so on. It was the same ancient mixture of smiles and threats, of promised favors if I "played the game," and of political destruction prophesied if I refused. I was so used to the thing by this time that I was no longer even indignant at it. I thanked my honest friend for his disinterested solicitude about my political welfare, and got rid of him.

The law in the Cronin case was clear. A community, under its police powers, has the right, in the interests of "public health, public morals and public welfare," to forbid women doing anything detrimental to those interests. The wine-room was an exercise of the police power. I so held in my decision, and I was sustained by the Supreme Court of Colorado and again by the Supreme Court of the United States when the penniless Cronin, represented by Milton Smith, appealed to those courts. You may wonder where Cronin got the money to carry on such expensive litigation. You would have understood his status in the matter if you had seen the look of reproachful bewilderment that he turned on his counsel when he heard my decision. It was as if he said: "Why, I thought this was only a stall! Where's your pull with this court? What sort of mess are you fellows trying to get me into?"

That was August, 1901, and the elections were to be held in November. "You're done," the politicians told me. "If you ever get the nomination, you'll be scratched off the ticket by the liberal element. Sure as shooting!"

I did not much care. I had had the satisfaction of getting one heavy whack in on the snout of the Beast, and I went back to my work for the children so as to establish at least a precedent of procedure for my successor to follow. But that work, and my decision in the Cronin case, had brought me to the notice of the "troublesome church element." It would have been poor politics to stand against the sweep of the reform wave in an attempt to prevent my renomination. So I was allowed a place on the Democratic ticket again, and the System prepared quietly to "knife" me and elect my Republican opponent.

At that time I was squeamish about judges "playing politics," and I decided that I should make no speeches and take no active part in the campaign. I had been assessed $1,000 by the finance committee as my contribution to the campaign fund, and an officer of the First National Bank of Denver (in which the court funds were deposited) offered to pay the assessment for me. I was no longer as innocent as I had been in the days of Gardner's first nomination, and I refused the offer and paid the money from my own purse. But it took all I had; I had nothing left even to pay for the printing of a circular letter to the electorate, and I allowed some lawyer friends to pay for that publication--a mistake which I have never made since.

As election day approached it became apparent to every politician that I was hopelessly "out of the running." My Republican opponent was speaking every night--particularly from the bars of saloons--to enthusiastic audiences. I was posted in every "dive" in Denver as the one man on the Democratic ticket who was not "right." Sample ballots were put up, showing how to scratch me. The Democratic workers, to whom I had refused the spoils of office in the County Court, were openly working against me. It was cheerfully predicted at Democratic headquarters that I could not possibly pull through, that I should run "away behind the ticket." After looking over the situation myself, I decided that I had not the shadow of a chance; and I went to bed early, on Election Night, without waiting to hear the returns.

It was not until the following morning, when I came down to breakfast, that I learned, from the newspaper reports, what had happened. The lower wards had "knifed" me unmercifully; but in the upper districts, among the homes, unexpected thousands had rallied to save the "kids' court," and rebuke the "wine-room gang." Instead of running behind my ticket, I had run 2000 votes ahead of it!

* * *

Meanwhile, we had been carrying on, also, our campaign against the jail, with the ultimate purpose of obtaining a detention home-school for children. I had found conditions in the jails almost as bad as they were in the dives. Boys repeated to me the obscene stories they had heard there, from the older prisoners, and described the abominable pollutions that had been committed on their little bodies. I learned from a boy sixteen years old, a confirmed criminal, that he had first been imprisoned when he was ten and that he had learned in jail how to crack safes and had practised that art successfully when he was fifteen; he told of it with pride, and with an admiration of the man who had taught him. He said it was his ambition now to kill a policeman whom he hated, and he had taken as his model in life a young outlaw named Harry Tracy whose exploits had been reported in the newspapers. I found that the boys were guilty of indecent practices among themselves and that, being confined in the matron's quarters, they had broken off the plaster of the wall that separated them from the women's room; and the girls there--it is unmentionable. Schoolboys they were. And when they were released, they went back to school, with the evil lessons they had learned, and taught them to their companions, spreading the plague, and infecting hundreds of young lives with the deadly virus of a physical vice.

In addition to all this I found that some of the police were guilty of cruelties to the boys, used language to them that is unreportable, and unconsciously taught the boys to hate the law and look upon us all as their enemies. Several boys complained to me that they had been beaten by the jailer, and I found on investigation that they had; the welts and bruises on their bodies showed it; and prisoners who had seen them beaten testified to it. One morning a boy, released from jail where he had been locked up on a suspicion that proved false, came running into my chambers in hysterics, with the most awful look of horror on his face, and poured out to me with sobs and frightened shudderings, the story of how the police had cursed and abused him, and of how the vagrants and criminals in the "bull pen," where he had been thrown, had spat upon him and maltreated him. I kept going to the Chief of Police with these complaints, and to Frank Adams, the president of the Police Board. And they kept replying that the boys were lying to me, and that I was "going batty" on the "kid question" and encouraging the "little devils" to resist the police.

Things went on this way until our juvenile bills came before the Legislature, and then the opposition of the Police Board and the System came to a head under Senator "Billy" Adams, a brother of Frank Adams, the president of the Police Board. Nothing was done openly. The Board, of course, objected to allowing our probation officers police powers, chiefly because we could then prevent the wine-room keepers from getting "protection" and paying for it; but such a reason for opposition could not be acknowledged. Instead, the bills were fought secretly in the committees and kept from a vote in the House by means of the same jugglery on the calendar that I had seen used before, on our "three-fourths jury" bill. After consulting with a friendly newspaper reporter named Harry Wilbur, of the *Rocky Mountain News,* I decided to "grandstand" again. Wilbur had been a police court reporter and knew conditions in the jails. I gave him an interview in which I described some of the cases I had seen and investigated, and I gave him a free hand to add any other "horrible an' revoltin' details" that he knew to be true.

The result was an article that took even *my* breath away when I read it next day on the front page of the newspaper. It was the talk of the town. It was certainly the talk of the Police Board; and Mr. Frank Adams talked to the reporters in a high voice, indiscreetly. He declared that the boys were liars, that I was "crazy," and that conditions in the jails were as good as they could be. This reply was exactly what we wished. I demanded an investigation. The Board professed to be willing, but set no date. We promptly set one *for* them--the following Thursday at two o'clock in my chambers at the Court House-- and I invited to the hearing Governor Peabody, Mayor Wright, fifteen prominent ministers in the city, the Police Board and some members of the City Council.

On Thursday morning--to my horror--I learned from a friendly Deputy Sheriff that the subpoenas I had ordered sent to a number of boys whom I knew as jail victims had not been served. I had no witnesses. And in three hours the hearing was to begin. I appealed to the Deputy Sheriff to help me. He admitted that he could not get the boys in less than two days. "Well then," I said, "for heaven's sake, get me Mickey."

And Mickey? Well, Mickey was known to fame as "the worst kid in town." As such, his portrait had been printed in the newspapers--posed with his shine-box over his shoulder, a cigarette in the corner of his grin, his thumbs under his suspenders at the shoulders, his feet crossed in an attitude of nonchalent youthful deviltry. He had been brought before me more than once on charges of truancy, and I had been using him in an attempt to organize a newsboys' association under the supervision of the court. Moreover, he had been one of the boys who had been beaten by the jailer, and I knew he would be grateful to me for defending him.

It was midday before the Sheriff brought him to me. "Mickey," I said, "I'm in trouble, and you've got to help me get out of it. You know I helped *you*."

"Betcher life yuh did, Judge," he said, "I'm wit yuh. W'at d' yuh want?"

I told him what I wanted--every boy that he could get, who had been in jail. "And they've got to be in this room by two o'clock. Can you do it?"

Mickey threw out his dirty little hand. "Sure I kin. Don't yuh worry, Judge. Get me a wheel--dhat's all."

I hurried out with him and got him a bicycle, and he flew off down Sixteenth Street on it, his legs so short that his feet could only follow the pedals half way around. I went back to my chambers to wait.

I trusted Mickey. He was the brightest street gamin that our court ever knew. Once we organized a baseball nine, with Mickey as captain, in his quarter of the town where the Irish boys were continually at war in the streets with the Jewish children of the district. We gave them uniforms and bats and balls, on condition that they stop smoking cigarettes and fighting. His nine became the "champines" of the town among boys of their age; and one day in court I congratulated Mickey on his victories. "Aw well, Judge," he said, "yuh see it's dhis way: half o' dhese kids is Irish an' half o' dhem 's Jews. An' yuh know when dh' Irish an'dhe Jews get togedher dhey kin lick anyt'ing dhat comes down dhe pike!" "How can that be," I asked him, "when there are nine boys in a baseball team? There must be more of one than the other." "No, dhere ain't neidher," he said. "Dhe pitcher's an Irish Jew an'dhe best kid in dhe bunch. Come here, Greeny." "Greeny" was a Greenstein and he was red-headed. If he was not an Irish Jew I don't know what he could have been!

Anyway, I knew that if Mickey could not get the

boys for me, no one could. I waited. As two o'clock approached, the ministers began to come into my room, one by one, and take seats in readiness. Mr. Wilson of the Police Board arrived to represent his fellow-commissioners. The Deputy District Attorney came, the president of the upper branch of the City Council came, Mayor Wright came, and even Governor Peabody came--but no boys! I felt like a man who had ordered a big dinner in a strange restaurant for a party of friends, and then found that he had not brought his purse. . . . I was just about to begin my apologies when I heard an excited patter of small feet on the stairs and the shuffle and crowding of Mickey's cohorts outside in the hall. I threw open the door. "I got 'em, Judge," Mickey cried.

He had them--to the number of about twenty. I shook him by the shoulder, speechless with relief. "I tol' yuh we'd stan' by yuh, Judge," he grinned.

He had the worst lot of little jailbirds that ever saw the inside of a county court, and he pointed out the gem of his collection proudly--"Skinny" a lad in his teens, who had been in jail twenty-two times! "All right, boys," I told them, "I don't know you all, but I'll take Mickey's word for you. You've all been in jail and you know what you do there--all the dirty things you hear and see and do yourselves. I want you to tell some gentlemen in here about it. Don't be scared. They're your friends the same as I am. The cops say you've been lying to me about the way things are down in the jails there, and I want you to tell the truth. Nothing but the truth, now. Mickey, you pick them out and send them in one by one--your best witnesses first."

I went back to my chambers. "Gentlemen," I said, "we're ready."

I sat down at the big table with the Governor at my right, the Mayor at my left and the president of the Board of Supervisors and Police Commissioner Wilson at either end of the table. The ministers seated themselves in the chairs about the room. (We allowed no newspaper reporters in, because I knew what sort of vile and unprintable testimony was coming.) Mickey sent in his first witness.

One by one, as the boys came, I impressed upon them the necessity of telling the truth, encouraged them to talk, and tried to put them at their ease. I started each by asking him how often he had been in jail, what he had seen there, and so forth. Then I sat back and let him tell his story.

And the things they told would raise your hair. I saw the blushes rise to the foreheads of some of the ministers at the first details. As we went on, the perspiration stood on their faces. Some sat pale, staring appalled at these freckled youngsters from whose little lips, in a sort of infantile eagerness to tell all they knew, there came stories of bestiality that were the more horrible because they were so innocently, so boldly, given. It was enough to make a man weep; and indeed tears of compassionate shame came to the eyes of more than one father there, as he listened. One boy broke down and cried when he told of the vile indecencies that had been committed upon him by the older criminals; and I saw the muscles working in the clenched jaws of some of our "investigating committee"-- saw them swallowing the lump in the throat--saw them looking down at the floor blinkingly, afraid of losing their self-control. The Police Commissioner made the mistake of cross-examining the first boy, but the frank answers he got only exposed worse matters. The boys came and came, till at last, a Catholic priest, Father O'Ryan, cried out: "My God! I have had enough!" Governor Peabody said hoarsely: "I never knew there was such immorality in *the world*!" Someone else put in, "It's awful--awful!" in a half groan.

"Gentlemen," I said, "there have been over two thousand Denver boys put through those jails and those conditions, in the last five years. Do you think it should go on any longer?"

Governor Peabody rose. "No," he said, "no. Never in my life have I heard of so much rot--corruption-- vileness--as I've heard here to-day from the mouths of these babies. I want to tell you that nothing I can do in my administration can be of more importance--nothing I can do will I do more gladly than sign those bills that Judge Lindsey is trying to get through the Legislature to do away with these terrible conditions. And if," he said, turning to the Police Commissioner, "Judge Lindsey is 'crazy,' I want my name written under his, among the *crazy* people. And if any one says these boys are 'liars,' that man is a liar himself!"

Phew! The "committee of investigation" dissolved, the boys trooped away noisily, and the ministers went back to their pulpits to voice the horror that had kept them silent in my small chamber of horrors for two hours. Their sermons went into the newspapers under large black headlines; and by the end of the next week our juvenile court bills were passed by the Legislature and made law in Colorado.

* * *

Through these two years of quarrelling and crusading, our court work for the children was going on very happily. It was a recreation for us all, and it kept me full of hope--for it was successful. We were getting the most unexpected results. We were learning something new every day. We were deducing, from what we learned, theories to be tested in daily practice, and then devising court methods by which to apply the theories that proved correct. It had all the fascination of a scientific research, of practical invention, and of a work of charity combined. It was a succession of surprises and a continual joy.

I had begun merely with a sympathy for children and a conviction that our laws against crime were as inapplicable to children as they would be to idiots. I soon realized that not only our laws but our whole system of criminal procedure was wrong. It was based upon fear; and fear, with children, as with their elders, is the father of lies. I found that when a boy was brought before me, I could do nothing with him until I had taken the fear out of his heart; but once I had gotten rid of that fear, I found--to my own amazement--that I could do anything with him. I could do things that seemed miraculous, especially to the police, who seldom tried anything but abuse and curses, and the more or less refined brutalities of the "sweat box" and the "third degree." I learned that instead of fear we must use sympathy, but without cant, without hypocrisy, and without sentimentalism. We must first convince the boy that we were his friends but the determined enemies of his misdeeds; that we wished to help him to do right, but could do nothing for him if he persisted in doing wrong. We had to encourage him to confess his wrongdoing, teach him wherein it had been wrongdoing, and strengthen him to do right thereafter.

I found--what so many others have found--that children are neither good nor bad, but either strong or weak. They are naturally neither moral nor immoral--but merely unmoral. They are little savages, living in a civilized society that has not yet civilized them, often at war with it, frequently punished by it, and always secretly in rebellion against it, until the influences of the home, the school and the church gradually overcome their natural savagery and make them moral and responsible members of society. The mistake of the criminal law had been to punish these little savages as if they had been civilized, and by so doing, in nine cases out of ten, make them criminal savages. Our work, we found, was to aid the civilizing forces--the home, the school, and the church--and to protect society by making the children good members of society instead of punishing them for being irresponsible ones. If we failed, and the child proved incorrigible, the criminal law could then be invoked. But the infrequency with which we failed was one of the surprises of the work.

Take, for example, the case of Lee Martin and his "River Front Gang." He was a boy burglar, a sneak thief, a pickpocket, a jail breaker, and a tramp; and his "gang" was known to the newspapers as the most desperate band of young criminals in Denver. Lee Martin and another member of the gang, named Jack Heimel, were one night caught in a drugstore into which they had broken; and

when I went to see them in jail, I found them strapped
to the benches in their cells, bruised and battered
from an interview with the police, in which they had
been punished for refusing to "snitch" (tell) on their
fellow-members of the gang. This was before the passage of our juvenile court laws and I wished to have an
opportunity to try what I could do with these two boys.
The police did not wish me to have them.

I told the boys that I intended to try to help
them, and they sneered at me. I told them that I
thought they had not been given a "square deal"--
which was true--but they did not respond. I used what
tact and sympathy I could to draw them out and get
their side of the story of their war with society, but
it took me something like a month of frequent visits
to get them to trust me and to believe that I wished to
help them. In the end I was successful. I got their
story--a story too long to repeat here; but it proved
to me that the boys had been as much sinned against
as sinning. They had begun as irresponsible little
savages, and they had been made desperate young
criminals. Their parents had failed to civilize them,
and the school and the church had never had an opportunity to try. I resolved to see if it was too late
to begin.

The police captain assured me that it was. "You
can't baby Lee Martin," he said. "He's been in jail
thirteen times, and it hasn't done him any good."

"Well, I'd like to see what we can do," I replied.
"If we fail, we'll still have twelve times the best
of the jail. It has cost this city, in officers' fees
alone, over a thousand dollars to make a criminal of
him. Let us see how much it will cost to turn him into an honest boy."

The officer reeled off a long list of Martin's
offences, and I retorted by showing a typewritten record of them, twice as long. "How in the world did
you get 'em, Judge?" he said. "We couldn't *sweat* 'em
out of him."

After a week of such argument, we got the case
referred to our court. The boys were tried; and, of

course, their guilt was clear. I sent them back to the jail under suspended sentence, and thought the matter over.

One night I had them brought to my chambers under guard, and after a talk with Heimel I sent him and the guard away, and concentrated on Martin. I decided to put my influence over him to the test. I told him of the fight I was making for him, showed him how I had been spending all my spare time "trying to straighten things out" for him and Heimel, and warned him that the police did not believe I could succeed. "Now, Lee," I said, "you can run away if you want to, and prove me a liar to the cops. But I want to help you, and I want you to stand by me. I want you to trust me, and I want you to go back to the jail there, and let me do the best I can."

He went. And he went alone--unguarded.

Then I put him and Heimel on probation, and in a few days they came to see me and brought "Red" Mike and Tommie Green, of the "River Front Gang." I talked to them about their offences against the law, and told them I wanted to help them do what was right and live honest lives, unpersecuted by the police; and I praised Martin for his moral strength in going back to the jail alone. Before they left me, "Red" and Tommie had "snitched" on themselves, and I had two new probationers. One by one the others followed, until I had all seven members of the gang on my list, all confessed wrong-doers pledging to give up crime and make an honest effort to be "straight." Six of the seven are to-day honest young workmen; Lee Martin failed, after a long and plucky fight, and is now in the penitentiary. "The River Front Gang," to my knowledge, has been responsible for the reformation of thirty boys in Denver; and Lee Martin, in his time, did more to discourage crime than any policeman in the city.

For example: one day a boy--whom I knew--stole a pocketbook from a woman in a department store. I told Lee that something ought to be done for that boy, and Lee brought him to me--from a cheap theatre where he had been "treating the gang." We worked on him together, and we straightened him up. He has since become a trusted employee in the very store in which he stole the pocketbook.

In another instance, I sent Lee after a boy, arrested for stealing a watch, who had sawed his way out of jail and had not been recaptured by the police. Lee got him--in El Paso--and brought him to me. After a talk with him, I gave him a twenty-dollar bill and sent him, alone, unshadowed, to redeem the watch, which he had pawned for $3. He returned with the watch and the $17 change. Then I persuaded him to return the watch to the man from whom he had stolen it, and, of course, the prosecution against him was dropped. We have never since had a complaint against the boy, although he had been one of the worst boy thieves in the city.

I could relate cases of this sort interminably. I *have* related them, in newspaper reviews, in magazine articles, and from the public platform. And I find that many people have misunderstood me and have accepted my statements as evidence that I have some sort of hypnotic power over boys and can make them do things contrary to their natures. I can not. I do nothing that any man or woman cannot do by the same method. It is the method that works the miracle--although, of course, no one in his senses will claim that the method never fails, that there are *no* cases in which force and punishment have to be used.

Another lesson about boys I learned from little "Mickey"--when I was investigating his charge that the jailer had beaten him. The jailer said: "Some o' those kids broke a window in there, and when I asked Mickey who it was he said he didn't know. O' course he knew. D' you think I'm goin' to have kids lie to me?" A police commissioner who was present turned to Mickey: "Mickey," he said, "why did you lie?" Mickey faced us, in his rags. "Say," he asked, "do yuh t'ink a fullah ought to snitch on a kid?" And the way he asked it made me ashamed of myself. Here was a quality of loyalty that we should be fostering in him instead of trying to crush out of him. It was the beginning, in the boy, of that feeling of responsibility to his fellows on which society is founded. Thereafter no child brought before our court was ever urged to turn state's evidence against his partners in crime--much less rewarded for doing so, or punished for refusing to do so. Each was encouraged to "snitch" on himself, and himself only.

Still another lesson I learned from an inveterate little runaway named Harry. After several attempts to reform him, I sentenced him to the Industrial School in Golden; and this being before the days of the Detention School, he was returned to the jail until a sheriff could "take him up." That night the jailer telephoned me that Harry was in hysterics, screaming in his cell and calling wildly to me to help him. "You'd better come down, Judge," the jailer said, "an' see if you can get him quiet." I went to the jail. Inside, the steel doors were opened and the steel bolts withdrawn, one by one, with a portentous clanking and grating. It was as if we were about to penetrate to some awful dungeon in which a murderous giant was penned--so formidable were the iron obstacles that were swung back before us and clashed shut on our heels. And when I reached, at the end of a guarded corridor, the barred door of Harry's cell, there, in the dim glow of a light overhead, the boy lay asleep on the floor, his round little legs drawn up, his head pillowed on his tiny arm, his baby face pale under the prison lamp. The sight was so pitifully ridiculous that I choked up at it. It seemed such a folly--such a cruel folly-- to lock up a child in such a place of lonely terror.

The jailer opened the cell door for me, and I began to raise the boy to put him on his prison "stretcher." His head fell back over my arm, like an infant's. He woke with a start and clutched me, in a return of the hysterical fear that had been mercifully forgotten in sleep. And then, when he recognized me, "Judge," he pleaded, "Judge. Gi' me another chance. I'll be good. Judge! Just once--once more. Judge!" I had to sit down beside him on the floor and try to reassure him.

I tried to be stern with him. I told him that I had trusted him and trusted him again and again; and he had failed me every time. I explained that we were sending him to the Industrial School for his own good, to make a "strong" boy of him; that he was "weak," untrustworthy. "I can *help* you, Harry," I said. "But you've got to carry yourself. If I let boys go when they do bad things, I'll lose my job. The people'll get another judge, in my place, to punish boys, if *I* don't do it. I can't let you go."

We went over it and over it; and at last I thought I had him feeling more resigned and cheerful, and I got up to leave him. But when I turned to the door, he fell to his knees before me and stretching out his little arms to me, his face distorted with tears, he cried: "Judge! Judge! If you let me go, *I'll never get you into trouble again!*"

I had him! It was the voice of loyalty. "Mac," I said to the jailer, "this boy goes with me. I'll write an order for his release."

I took him to his home that night, but his mother did not wish to have him back. Her husband had deserted her; she worked all day in a hotel kitchen; she could not take proper care of her boy, and she was afraid that he would be killed on some of his long "bumming" trips in the freight cars. But she finally consented to give him another trial; and this time he "stuck." "Judge," she told me long afterward, "I asked Harry, the other day, how it was he was so good for *you*, when he wouldn't do it for me or the policeman. And he says: 'Well, maw, you see if I gets bad agin, the Judge he'll lose his job. I've got to stay with him, 'cause he stayed with me.'" I have used that appeal to loyalty hundreds of times since, in our work with the boys, and it is almost infallibly successful.

I saw, too, from Harry's case, that if we were to reform children we must help parents who were unable to keep a close watch on their children. And nowadays if one of our probationers fails to arrive at school, the teacher is required to telephone the Juvenile

Court immediately, and a probation officer starts out at once to find the delinquent. Every two weeks, on "report day," the probationers must bring us reports on their behaviour from the school, the home and the neighbourhood; and by praising those who have good reports and censuring those who have bad ones, we are not only able to prevent wrong-doing but to encourage right-doing. We impress on the children the need of doing right because it *is* right, because it "hurts to do wrong," because only "weak kids" do wrong--*not* because wrong is punished; for *that* teaching, I believe, is the great error of our ethics. The fear of punishment, I find, makes weak children liars and hypocrites, and, with strong ones, it adds to the enticement of evil all the proverbial sweetness of the forbidden fruit.

During the first two years of our work, 554 children were put on probation; only 31 were ever returned to the court again, and of these 31 a number were returned and sent to Golden because of the hopelessness of reforming them in their squalid homes.

One evening a probationer brought four boys to my chambers with the announcement that they wished to "snitch" on themselves. They had been stealing bicycles--making a regular practice of it--and they had five such thefts to their discredit. I investigated their story and found it to be true. The police had a complete record of the thefts, and I tried--and got the boys to try--to recover the wheels, but we could not; they had been sold and resold and quite lost track of. A police officer, with whom I consulted, insisted that the boys should be arrested and sentenced to jail; and while I listened to him it dawned upon me what the difference was between the criminal procedure and the methods of the court. "Officer," I said, "you are trying to save bicycles. I am trying to save boys. The boys are more important than the bicycles. And if we can save the boys we can save bicycles in the future that we could not save in the past." I put the boys on probation, with the understanding that if they did not live up to their new resolve to be honest, I should be allowed to use their confessions against them. Not one of them failed me. The court helped them to get work and they are honest and useful members of society to-day.

In one year 201 boys came in this way to our court, voluntarily, and confessed their wrong-doing, and promised to "cut it out."

One evening, after I had adjourned court and the room had emptied, I saw a youngster sitting in a chair by the rear wall, apparently forgotten by his parents. He was no bigger than a baby. I sent the bailiff to ask him if he knew his name or address. He came up to the bench--to my chair on the platform--and hiding his face against my shoulder he began to cry. He had been "swipin' things," he said, and wanted to "cut it out." And would I give him a chance--as I had another boy he knew? We gave him a chance. He reported regularly, for more than a year, and proved to be an honest, sturdy boy. Another boy who came to my chambers with a similar confession was so small that I said to him, "You're a mighty little boy. How did you find your way down here?" "Well," he replied, "most every kid I seed knew the way." I found that nearly all these boys were members of neighbourhood "gangs," that some member of the gang had been in court, had gone back to the gang with the lessons we had tried to teach him and had used his influence to send other boys to us. We began to reach for this gang spirit and to turn it to our uses instead of against us; and we succeeded there, too, in time. I could relate scores of stories that came to us of how the gangs threatened to "beat up" some young delinquent if he did not play "square with the Judge." We taught the boys who had been doing wrong that they should try to "overcome the evil" they had done, by now doing something good; and they practised that doctrine by persuading their companions to desist from some mischief they had planned.

I even had a little newsboy come to me with the assurance that if I wanted the "street kids" to stop "shooting craps," I need only go down and tell them so. "Dhere ain't a kid in the whole push," he said, "dhat won't go down the line wit' yuh, Judge. Dhe cops can't make 'em stop craps, but I bet dhey'd do it fer *you*." I did not try it. I did not believe that I could permanently stop street boys shooting craps; it is as natural for them to gamble as for schoolboys to play marbles. But I rejoiced in the loyalty, the spirit of cooperation, shown by these street gamins. Therein lies the success of the Juvenile Court.

In the days before we got our Detention School any boy sentenced to the Industrial School at Golden had to be returned to the jail to wait until a deputy sheriff could "take him up." I found that the deputies were keeping the boys in jail until there were several under sentence, and then making one trip and charging the county mileage on each boy. Petty graft again! And conditions in the jail were as I have already described them.

I tried to make the deputies take the boys separately, immediately after sentence; but I did not succeed. The grafters were protected by politicians, and I was powerless. "Very well," I said, "I'll see whether I cannot send these boys to Golden alone, without any guard, and cut out your fees entirely." And I succeeded.

I took each boy into my chambers and told him that I wanted him to go to Golden . "Now," I would say to him, "if you think I'm making a mistake in trying to save you--if you think you're not worth saving-- don't go. Run away, if you feel that way about it. I can't help you if you don't want to help yourself. You've been a weak boy. You've been doing bad things. I want you to be a strong boy and do what's right. We don't send boys to Golden to punish them. We do it to help them. They give you a square deal out there-- teach you a trade so you can earn an honest living and look anybody in the face. I'm not going to bring a deputy in here and handcuff you and have you taken away like *that*. Here are your commitment papers. Go yourself and go alone--or don't go at all if you don't think I'm trying to help you and sending you there for your own good." And invariably, the boy went. In eight years, out of 507 cases, I had only five failures. One of these was a boy who thought he was being followed and who ran away instinctively "to beat the game." Another was a boy who confessed that he couldn't "make it," because the route to Golden led him past his old "stamping grounds"; and when I gave him tickets over another route, he made the trip successfully. A third was an hysterical youngster who got as far as the railroad station with an older lad, but broke down there and could not go on. None of the failures were outright; and none of the boys were lost. (During these eight years, the police, I was told, lost forty-two "breakaways" who were never recovered.) And we saved the county several thousand dollars in mileage fees.

One boy, whom the police considered the worst little runaway in town, took his papers and delivered himself at Golden while the police waited, with expectant grins, to hear that he had made off; and those police were so sure he would fail me that they had two reporters "tipped off" to watch the case and write it up. I have had a young burglar, on trial, escape from the court room and evade the police--only to come to my house at midnight and surrender himself to me, because his gang had told him that I would "be square" with him if he was "square" with me. And not only children have gone alone to jail. Grown men whom I have found guilty of "contributory delinquency" have done the same thing, satisfied that they had broken the laws and should bear the penalty.

This achievement of our Juvenile Court has attracted more attention than anything else we have done; and yet it is not an isolated act; it is merely one of the results of the method. The criminal law is founded on vengeance. It treats all criminals as born criminals, incorrigible and unforgivable. It is designed to save property, not to save men; and it does neither: it makes more criminals than it crushes. I believe that the methods of our Juvenile Court could be applied to half the criminal cases on our calendars.

The majority of our criminals are not born, but made--
and ill-made. They can be re-made as easily as the
"River Front Gang" was re-made if we would use the
methods of Christianity on them and not those of a
sort of fiendish paganism that exacts "an eye for an
eye," and exacts it in a spirit of vengeance.

SELECTED BIBLIOGRAPHY

Bromfield, Louis, *Colorado* (New York, 1947)

Fowler, Gene, *Timberline* (New York, 1933)

Hafen, Leroy R., *Colorado and its People* (Chicago, 4 vol., 1948)

Hafen, Leroy R., *Colorado Gold Rush* (Glendale, Calif., 1941)

Willard, James F., and Colin B. Goodykoontz, *Experiments in Colorado Colonization, 1869-1872* (Boulder, 1926)

Willison, George F., *Here They Dug Gold* (New York, 1931)

INDEX
(Names in Chronology)

Adams, Alva, 13
Archuleta, Antonio D., 11
Arthur, Chester A., 12

Bent, Charles, 2
Bent, George, 2
Bent, Robert, 2
Bent, William, 2, 7
Buchanan, James, 4
Byers, William N., 3

Carpenter, Scott, 16
Carson, Kit, 11
Chaffee, Jerome B., 10
Crowley, John H., 13
Custer, George, 9

Denver, James W., 2
Douglas, Stephen A., 4

Eisenhower, Dwight D., 15
Elbert, Samuel H., 8
Escalante, Francisco, 1
Evans, John, 5

Fremont, John Charles, 4

Garfield, James A., 10
Gilpin, William, 4, 5
Grant, Ulysses S., 9
Gregory, John, 3
Gunnison, J. W., 2, 9

Hill, Nathaniel, 7
Hinsdale, George A., 8

Jackson, Andrew, 13
Jackson, George A., 3
James, Edwin, 1
Jefferson, Thomas, 4
Johnson, Andrew, 6

Larimer, William, 5
Lincoln, Abraham, 11
Lindsey, Ben B., 13
Logan, John A., 11
Long, Stephen H., 1
Lupton, Madeiro Gonzales, 1

Mallet brothers, 1
Meeker, Nathan C., 10
Moffat, David H., 13
Morgan, Christopher A., 11

Otero, Miguel, 11

Palmer, William J., 8
Phillips, R. O., 11
Pike, Zebulon M., 1
Pitkin, Frederick W., 10
Prowers, John W., 11

Roman Nose, Chief, 7
Routt, John L., 9

Scott, Sir Walter, 10
Sedgwick, John, 11
St. Vrain, Cerean, 2
Steele, R. W., 3, 4

Teller, Henry M., 12

Ulibarri, Juan, 1

Washington, George, 11
Weld, Lewis L., 5
Wooton, "Uncle Dick," 2